Christmas CHEER

Recipes and Party Ideas

From elegant dinners to casual get-togethers, holiday parties bring a special sparkle to Christmas. We rediscover the wondrous joy of the season as family and friends join to celebrate with laughter and merriment. Amid the whirl of holiday socials, we often find that certain gatherings stand out as truly memorable occasions — times to treasure for years to come.

To help with your party planning, we've created this imaginative collection of entertaining ideas. As you turn the pages, you'll discover a host of bright inspirations, with menus and decorations for every age and every style. There are traditional holiday gatherings, along with a few adventurous themes that are just for fun. Many of them can be adapted for other occasions, too! We hope that this volume will add an extra measure of cheer to your holiday parties.

Anne Childs

LEISURE ARTS, INC.
Little Rock, Arkansas

Christmas CHEER

Recipes and Party Ideas

EDITORIAL STAFF

Editor-in-Chief: Anne Van Wagner Childs
Executive Director: Sandra Graham Case
Executive Editor: Susan Frantz Wiles
Publications Director: Carla Bentley
Creative Art Director: Gloria Bearden
Production Art Director: Melinda Stout

TECHNICAL
Managing Editor: Sherry Taylor O'Connor
Senior Editor: Kathy Rose Bradley
Senior Technical Writer: Kimberly J. Smith
Technical Writers: Ann Brawner Turner and
  Chanda English Adams

DESIGN
Design Director: Patricia Wallenfang Sowers
Designers: Diana Heien Suttle, Linda Diehl Tiano,
  Donna Waldrip Pittard, and Rebecca Sunwall Werle

FOODS
Foods Editor: Susan Warren Reeves, R.D.
Consulting Foods Editor: Celia Fahr Harkey, R.D.
Assistant Foods Editor: Jane Kenner Prather
Test Kitchen Assistant: Nora Faye Spencer Clift

EDITORIAL
Senior Editor: Linda L. Trimble
Senior Editorial Writer: Laurie S. Rodwell

ART
Book/Magazine Art Director: Diane M. Ghegan
Senior Production Artist: Michael A. Spigner
Production Artists: Roberta Aulwes, Sarah J.
  Dearworth, Hubrith E. Esters, Kenny L. Gipson,
  Sonya McFatrich, Guniz Ustun, and Karen L. Wilson
Creative Art Assistant: Judith Howington Merritt
Photography Stylists: Karen Smart Hall and
  Christina Tiano
Typesetters: Cindy Lumpkin and Stephanie Cordero

ADVERTISING AND DIRECT MAIL
Associate Editor: Dorothy Latimer Johnson
Copywriters: Steven M. Cooper, Marla Shivers,
  and Tena Kelley Vaughn
Designer: Rhonda H. Hestir
Art Director: Jeff Curtis
Production Artist: Linda Lovette Smart

BUSINESS STAFF

Publisher: Steve Patterson
Controller: Tom Siebenmorgen
Retail Sales Director: Richard Tignor
Retail Marketing Director: Pam Stebbins
Retail Customer Services Director: Margaret Sweetin
Marketing Manager: Russ Barnett

Executive Director of Marketing and Circulation:
  Guy A. Crossley
Fulfillment Manager: Byron L. Taylor
Print Production: Nancy Reddick Lister and
  Laura Lockhart

MEMORIES IN THE MAKING SERIES

Copyright© 1993 by Leisure Arts, Inc., 5701 Ranch Drive, Little Rock, Arkansas 72212. All rights reserved. No part of this book may be reproduced in any form or by any means without the prior written permission of the publisher, except for brief quotations in reviews appearing in magazines or newspapers. We have made every effort to ensure that these recipes and instructions are accurate and complete. We cannot, however, be responsible for human error, typographical mistakes, or variations in individual work. Printed in the United States of America. First Printing.

Library of Congress Catalog Number 93-78285
International Standard Book Number 0-942237-28-5

Table of Contents

Table of Contents

Table of Contents

MERRY COOKIE SWAP

An old-fashioned cookie swap is a tasty way to share Christmas spirit with friends. Everyone brings along a batch or two of their favorite cookies — enough for each guest to take some home in a decorated market basket that you provide. Along with the handmade invitations, you'll want to include coordinating recipe cards so guests can bring copies of their recipes to share. Our delectable cookie assortment is perfect for refreshments!

Cashew Crescents

Pecan-Caramel Brownies

Raspberry Fudgies

Chocolate-Orange Balls

Coffee Lace Cookies

Crunchy Pecan Cookies

Cinnamon Fingers

Chocolate Crisp Cookies

Snowflake Meringue Cookies

Wafer Roll Cookies

Macadamia Shortbreads

Sesame Cookies

6

you're invited
to a

cookie swap!

CASHEW CRESCENTS

¾ cup butter, softened
½ cup granulated sugar
1 egg yolk
1½ cups all-purpose flour
1 cup finely chopped dry-roasted cashews
Sifted confectioners sugar

Preheat oven to 350 degrees. In a medium bowl, cream butter and sugar until fluffy. Add egg yolk; stir until smooth. Add flour and cashews; stir until a soft dough forms. Shape tablespoonfuls of dough into crescent shapes and place 1 inch apart on a greased baking sheet. Bake 12 to 15 minutes or until edges are light brown. While cookies are still warm, coat with confectioners sugar. Transfer to a wire rack to cool completely. Coat with confectioners sugar again. Store in an airtight container.

Yield: about 3 dozen cookies

PECAN-CARAMEL BROWNIES

1 box (21½ ounces) brownie mix
½ cup water
¼ cup vegetable oil
1 egg
1 bag (14 ounces) caramel candies
2 tablespoons milk
1 package (6 ounces) semisweet chocolate chips
1 cup chopped pecans, divided

Preheat oven to 350 degrees. In a medium bowl, combine brownie mix, water, oil, and egg; mix just until moistened. Spread one-half of batter in a greased 9 x 13-inch baking pan. Bake 10 minutes.

In a small saucepan, combine caramels and milk. Stirring occasionally, cook over medium heat until smooth. Remove from heat. Sprinkle chocolate chips and ½ cup pecans over partially baked batter. Drizzle caramel mixture over pecans. Spread remaining batter over caramel mixture. Sprinkle remaining ½ cup pecans over batter. Bake 35 to 40 minutes or until edges begin to pull away from sides of pan. Cool completely in pan. Cut into squares. Store in an airtight container.

Yield: about 3 dozen brownies

RASPBERRY FUDGIES

CRUST

½ cup butter or margarine
2 ounces unsweetened baking chocolate, chopped
1 cup granulated sugar
2 eggs
⅛ teaspoon raspberry-flavored oil (used in candy making)
½ cup all-purpose flour
½ cup chopped pecans
1 tablespoon vanilla extract

TOPPING

¼ cup raspberry jelly
1 cup granulated sugar
⅓ cup evaporated milk
2 tablespoons butter or margarine
½ cup semisweet chocolate chips
¼ cup marshmallow creme
1 tablespoon vanilla extract
1 cup chopped pecans

Preheat oven to 350 degrees. For crust, melt butter and chocolate over low heat in a small saucepan, stirring constantly. Remove from heat. In a medium bowl, beat sugar and eggs until foamy. Gradually add chocolate mixture and raspberry-flavored oil; beat until smooth. Stir in flour, pecans, and vanilla. Spoon batter into a greased 9 x 13-inch baking dish. Bake 25 to 30 minutes or until set in center.

For topping, spread jelly evenly over warm crust; cool completely. In a medium saucepan, combine sugar, milk, and butter. Stirring occasionally, bring to a boil over medium heat. Stirring constantly, boil 5 minutes. Remove from heat. Add chocolate chips, marshmallow creme, and vanilla; stir until smooth. Stir in pecans. Immediately pour topping over jelly. Cool completely in pan. Cut into 1-inch squares. Store in an airtight container.

Yield: about 8 dozen fudgies

CHOCOLATE-ORANGE BALLS

1 package (12 ounces) semisweet chocolate chips
1½ cups vanilla wafer crumbs
¾ cup sifted confectioners sugar
½ cup sour cream
2 teaspoons dried grated orange peel
¼ teaspoon salt
10 pieces orange slice gumdrop candy, cut into quarters
Sifted confectioners sugar

Stirring constantly, melt chocolate chips in a large saucepan over low heat. Remove from heat; stir in cookie crumbs, sugar, sour cream, orange peel, and salt. Cover and chill until firm. Press crumb mixture around each piece of candy, forming 1½-inch balls. Coat with confectioners sugar. Store in an airtight container.

Yield: 40 balls

This cute tree is perfect for the kitchen! Nestled in a flour sack, the little evergreen is trimmed with Cookie Cutter Ornaments, braided jute, bows, wooden spoons, metal measuring cups, and other kitchen utensils.

9

Coffee Lace Cookies, coated with chocolate on one side, are just one of the many delicious types of cookies you can serve to keep guests from nibbling their take-home goodies.

COFFEE LACE COOKIES

    1 cup finely chopped pecans
    2 tablespoons instant coffee granules
    2 tablespoons hot water
    ½ cup butter, softened
    ½ cup firmly packed brown sugar
    2 tablespoons whipping cream
    ¼ cup all-purpose flour
    ¼ teaspoon salt
    ⅛ teaspoon baking soda
    1 cup quick-cooking rolled oats
   12 ounces semisweet baking
        chocolate, chopped

Preheat oven to 350 degrees. To toast pecans, spread evenly on an ungreased baking sheet and bake 5 to 8 minutes, stirring once. Cool completely on pan.

In a small bowl, dissolve coffee granules in water. In a large bowl, cream butter and sugar until fluffy. Beat in coffee mixture. In a small saucepan, heat cream over medium heat until boiling. Reduce heat to medium-low and simmer 2 to 3 minutes. Add cream to coffee mixture and stir until well blended. In a small bowl, combine flour, salt, and baking soda. Stir dry ingredients into creamed mixture. Stir in oats and pecans. Drop heaping teaspoonfuls of batter 4 inches apart onto a greased baking sheet. Use fingers to press each cookie into a 2-inch circle. Bake 8 minutes (cookies will be soft); cool on pan 3 minutes. Transfer to a wire rack to cool completely.

Stirring constantly, melt chocolate over low heat in a small saucepan. Spread chocolate over bottom of each cookie. Return to wire rack, chocolate side up. Allow chocolate to harden. Store in an airtight container in a cool dry place.

Yield: about 3½ dozen cookies

CRUNCHY PECAN COOKIES

    1 cup butter or margarine, softened
    1 cup granulated sugar
    1 cup firmly packed brown sugar
    1 cup vegetable oil
    1 egg
    1 teaspoon vanilla extract
   3½ cups all-purpose flour
    1 teaspoon baking soda
    ½ teaspoon salt
    2 cups finely crushed corn flake
        cereal
   1½ cups chopped pecans

Preheat oven to 350 degrees. In a large bowl, cream butter and sugars until fluffy. Beat in oil, egg, and vanilla. In a medium bowl, combine flour, baking soda, and salt. Add dry ingredients to creamed mixture; stir until a soft dough forms. Stir in cereal crumbs and pecans. Drop tablespoonful of dough 2 inches apart onto a greased baking sheet. Using a fork dipped in water, make a crisscross design on each cookie. Bake 10 to 12 minutes or until edges are light brown. Transfer to a wire rack to cool completely. Store in an airtight container.

Yield: about 7 dozen cookies

CINNAMON FINGERS

½ cup granulated sugar
½ teaspoon ground cinnamon
1 cup butter, softened
½ cup firmly packed brown sugar
1 teaspoon vanilla extract
2 cups all-purpose flour
1 cup finely ground pecans
¼ teaspoon salt

Preheat oven to 350 degrees. In a small bowl, combine granulated sugar and cinnamon; set aside.

In a medium bowl, cream butter, brown sugar, and vanilla until fluffy. Stir in flour, pecans, and salt. Shape dough into 3-inch-long rolls. Place each roll in sugar mixture and spoon sugar mixture over until well coated. Place on a greased baking sheet. Bake 15 to 18 minutes or until light brown. Transfer to a wire rack to cool completely. Store in an airtight container.

Yield: about 4½ dozen cookies

CHOCOLATE CRISP COOKIES

3 cups (one 12-ounce and one 6-ounce package) semisweet chocolate chips, divided
½ cup butter or margarine, softened
1½ cups granulated sugar
4 eggs
1 tablespoon vanilla extract
½ teaspoon chocolate extract
1 cup sifted all-purpose flour
1 teaspoon baking powder
¼ teaspoon salt

Preheat oven to 350 degrees. Stirring constantly, melt 1 cup chocolate chips over low heat in a small saucepan. Remove from heat. In a medium bowl, cream butter and sugar until fluffy. Add melted chocolate chips, eggs, and extracts; beat until smooth. In a small

Light and delicate, Snowflake Meringue Cookies are a lovely treat for cookie lovers. The confections are flavored with almond and cinnamon and piped into a snowflake pattern using a pastry bag.

bowl, combine flour, baking powder, and salt. Add dry ingredients to creamed mixture; stir until a soft dough forms. Stir in remaining 2 cups chocolate chips. Drop tablespoonfuls of dough 2 inches apart onto a greased baking sheet. Bake 15 to 17 minutes or until cookies are cracked on top. Immediately place on a wire rack to cool completely. Allow baking sheet to cool completely between batches. Store in an airtight container.

Yield: about 5 dozen cookies

SNOWFLAKE MERINGUE COOKIES

4 egg whites
1½ cups sifted confectioners sugar
1 teaspoon almond extract
½ teaspoon ground cinnamon
½ teaspoon cream of tartar
White crystal sugar

Trace pattern onto tracing paper. Cover greased baking sheets with waxed paper.

In a large bowl, beat egg whites until foamy. Add confectioners sugar, almond extract, cinnamon, and cream of tartar; beat until very stiff. Spoon meringue into a pastry bag fitted with a small star tip. For each cookie, place pattern under waxed paper and use as a guide to pipe meringue onto waxed paper. Sprinkle with crystal sugar. Allow cookies to sit at room temperature 30 minutes.

Preheat oven to 200 degrees. Bake 2 hours. Leaving cookies on waxed paper, remove waxed paper from baking sheet while cookies are still warm; cool completely. Carefully peel away waxed paper. Store in an airtight container.

Yield: about 2½ dozen cookies

Cookie Swap Baskets adorned with festive ribbon and Cookie Cutter Ornaments hold bags of cookies for guests to carry home. The country ornaments are easy to create by dressing up purchased cookie cutters with fabric-covered poster board, buttons, and bows. They're great for decorating the tree, too!

WAFER ROLL COOKIES

½ cup butter or margarine, softened
½ cup granulated sugar
½ cup all-purpose flour
2 egg whites
1 teaspoon vanilla extract
3 ounces semisweet baking
    chocolate, chopped
½ cup finely chopped pecans

Preheat oven to 400 degrees. In a medium bowl, cream butter and sugar until fluffy. Stir in flour. In a small bowl, beat egg whites until foamy. Beat egg whites and vanilla into creamed mixture. Drop teaspoonfuls of dough 4 inches apart onto a heavily greased baking sheet; flatten slightly. Bake 5 to 6 minutes or until edges are light brown. While cookies are still warm, roll each cookie around the end of a wooden spoon. Transfer to a wire rack, seam side down, to cool completely.

Stirring constantly, melt chocolate over low heat in a small saucepan. Dip ends of each cookie in chocolate and then in pecans. Return to wire rack; allow chocolate to harden. Store in an airtight container.

Yield: about 3 dozen cookies

MACADAMIA SHORTBREADS

2 cups all-purpose flour
2 jars (7 ounces each) whole
    macadamia nuts, divided
¼ teaspoon salt
1 cup butter, softened
½ cup firmly packed brown sugar
1 teaspoon vanilla extract

Preheat oven to 350 degrees. In a blender or food processor, process flour, 1 cup macadamia nuts, and salt until finely ground. In a medium bowl, cream next 3 ingredients until fluffy. Stir in flour mixture. Shape into 1-inch balls and place 2 inches apart on a greased baking sheet. Press 1 macadamia nut into center of each cookie. Bake 12 to 15 minutes or until edges are light brown. Cool completely on a wire rack.

Yield: about 5 dozen cookies

SESAME COOKIES

   1 cup all-purpose flour
   ½ cup sifted confectioners sugar
   ½ cup cornstarch
   1 cup butter, softened
   ¼ cup sesame seeds, toasted

In a medium bowl, combine flour, sugar, and cornstarch. Using a pastry blender or 2 knives, cut butter into dry ingredients until mixture resembles coarse meal. Knead on a lightly floured surface until a soft dough forms. Shape into a 12-inch-long roll. Coat with sesame seeds. Wrap in plastic wrap and refrigerate 1 hour.

Preheat oven to 300 degrees. Cut dough into ¼-inch-thick slices and place on a greased baking sheet. Bake 20 to 25 minutes or until edges are light brown. Cool completely on a wire rack.

Yield: about 3½ dozen cookies

COOKIE SWAP BASKET

For basket (page 12), you will need a large basket with handle, brown craft paper, 1¼"w craft ribbon, satin ribbon, desired Cookie Cutter Ornament (this page), ⅝"w paper-backed fusible web, hot glue gun, and glue sticks.

1. Glue craft ribbon around basket rim. Use satin ribbon to tie ornament to basket handle.
2. For basket liner, cut desired size square of craft paper. Cut 4 craft ribbon lengths and 8 web strips the same length as 1 edge of paper square.
3. Press each ribbon length in half lengthwise.

4. For 1 edge of liner, follow manufacturer's instructions to fuse 1 length of web tape along edge of paper. Do not remove paper backing. Turn paper over and fuse a second web length along same edge. Remove paper backing from both lengths. Insert webbed edge of paper into fold of 1 ribbon length; fuse in place. Repeat for remaining edges.

COOKIE CUTTER ORNAMENTS

For each ornament (page 12), you will need a cookie cutter; fabric; poster board; paper-backed fusible web; hot glue gun; glue sticks; and contrasting fabric for smaller cutouts, buttons, and craft glue (optional).

1. Cut 1 piece each of fabric and poster board slightly larger than cookie cutter. Follow manufacturer's instructions to fuse web to wrong side of fabric. Fuse fabric to poster board.
2. Place cookie cutter front side down on poster board side of fabric. Use a pen to draw around inside of cookie cutter; cut out shape.
3. If desired, cut a smaller cutout such as a heart or a tree from contrasting fabric. Use craft glue to glue cutout and/or buttons to front of cookie cutter shape.
4. Trimming edges if necessary, insert shape into front of cookie cutter. Keeping shape flush with front of cookie cutter, hot glue to secure.

INVITATIONS AND RECIPE CARDS

For invitations and recipe cards (pages 6 and 7), you will need cream-colored cover stock paper; fabrics; paper-backed fusible web; tracing paper; graphite transfer paper; black

and red permanent felt-tip pens with fine points; white paint pen with fine point; and peach, red, brown, and black colored pencils.

INVITATIONS

1. For Santa, trace entire pattern, page 114, onto tracing paper; do not cut out. Trace body, hat, and arm portions of pattern separately onto tracing paper; cut out.
2. For each invitation, cut a 5½"x 8½" piece of cream paper. Matching short edges, fold paper in half.
3. Use transfer paper to transfer entire Santa pattern to front of invitation.
4. Follow manufacturer's instructions to fuse web to wrong side of fabric.
5. Place body, hat, and arm patterns right side down on paper side of fabric. Use a permanent pen to draw around patterns. Cut out fabric just outside pen lines.
6. Fuse body, hat, and arm pieces to invitation.
7. Use black pen to draw over remaining transferred lines. Use colored pencils to color face, hand, cheek, cookie, and boots. Use paint pen to color beard, details on cookie, and pom-pom on hat.
8. Use black pen to write "You're invited to a cookie swap!" on invitation.

RECIPE CARDS

1. For each recipe card, cut a 3" x 5" piece of cream paper.
2. Use black pen to write "A recipe for" and "From" in top left corner of card.
3. For tree, follow manufacturer's instructions to fuse web to wrong side of fabric. Cut a small triangle from fabric and fuse to card. Use black pen to draw trunk.
4. Use red pen and a ruler to draw lines on card ¼" apart.

CHRISTMAS IN THE FOREST

Inspired by the beauty of the forest, this rustic dinner setting takes us back to olden days when chopping down the Christmas tree was an exciting event for the whole family. You can relive those times by inviting some friends to come along on your Christmas tree hunt or on a walk in the winter woods. Afterwards, our hearty dinner menu is sure to satisfy hungry appetites! Set in woodsy greens with vivid red accents, the table brings an outdoorsy feeling to your celebration. Completing the scene are handmade decorations like napkin rings and candles trimmed with twigs and berries and a patterned table runner.

Salisbury Venison Steaks

Zucchini with Basil Butter

Creamed Potatoes

Oatmeal Bread

Cranberry-Apple Turnovers

15

Made from ground venison and pork, Salisbury Venison Steaks are smothered with savory mushroom and onion gravy. For simple but delicious side dishes, serve buttery Creamed Potatoes and crisp-tender Zucchini with Basil Butter. Hearty Oatmeal Bread is a satisfying accompaniment to the meal.

SALISBURY VENISON STEAKS

1½ pounds ground venison
½ pound lean ground pork
1 egg, beaten
½ cup milk
½ cup plain bread crumbs
½ cup finely chopped onion
2 tablespoons dried parsley
2 teaspoons salt
1 teaspoon garlic powder
½ teaspoon ground black pepper
½ teaspoon dried oregano leaves
  All-purpose flour
⅓ cup plus 1 tablespoon vegetable
  oil, divided

1 large onion, sliced into rings
2 jars (4½ ounces each) sliced
  mushrooms, drained
2 tablespoons all-purpose flour
1 can (14½ ounces) beef broth

In a large bowl, combine first 11 ingredients. Shape into 10 patties; thoroughly coat each patty with flour.

Preheat oven to 300 degrees. In a large skillet, heat ⅓ cup oil over medium-high heat. Add steaks in batches and cook until brown on both sides. Reserving drippings, transfer steaks to a greased roasting pan. Place onion and mushrooms over steaks.

To make gravy, add remaining 1 tablespoon oil to meat drippings in skillet. Stir in 2 tablespoons flour and cook over medium heat until flour begins to brown. Stirring constantly, add beef broth and cook until slightly thickened. Pour gravy over steaks, cover, and bake 1 hour or until juices run clear when meat is pierced with a fork. Serve with gravy.

Yield: 10 steaks

CREAMED POTATOES

2½ pounds red potatoes, peeled
  and cut into bite-size pieces
¼ cup butter or margarine
3 tablespoons all-purpose flour
1 teaspoon salt
½ teaspoon ground black pepper
½ teaspoon garlic powder
2 cups milk

Place potatoes in a large saucepan and cover with salted water. Bring to a boil and cook until potatoes are tender; drain in a colander.

In same saucepan, melt butter over medium heat. Whisking constantly, add next 4 ingredients and cook 1 minute. Whisking constantly, gradually add milk and cook until thickened. Add potatoes and stir until well coated. Serve warm.

Yield: about 8 servings

ZUCCHINI WITH BASIL BUTTER

½ cup butter or margarine
1 cup fresh basil leaves, finely
  chopped *or* 2 tablespoons
  dried basil leaves, crushed
2 pounds zucchini, cut into
  2-inch-long thin strips
½ teaspoon salt
¼ teaspoon ground black pepper

In a large skillet, melt butter over medium heat. Add basil and cook 1 minute if using fresh or 3 minutes if using dried. Add zucchini; cook 3 to 4 minutes longer. Stir in salt and pepper. Serve warm.

Yield: about 8 servings

Flavorful Cranberry-Apple Turnovers are easy to make using purchased puff pastry. Cinnamon and nutmeg add festive spice to the sweet, tart filling. Twigs, berries, and greenery adorn the Rustic Napkin Rings.

OATMEAL BREAD

- 1 package dry yeast
- ¼ teaspoon granulated sugar
- 1 cup warm water
- 2 cups all-purpose flour
- ½ cup whole-wheat flour
- ⅔ cup plus 2 tablespoons old-
  fashioned rolled oats, divided
- ¼ cup nonfat dry milk
- 1 teaspoon salt
- ⅓ cup honey
- 2 tablespoons butter or margarine,
  melted
  Vegetable cooking spray

In a small bowl, dissolve yeast and sugar in water. In a large bowl, combine flours, ⅓ cup oats, milk, and salt. Add yeast mixture, honey, and butter to dry ingredients. Stir until a soft dough forms. Turn onto a lightly floured surface and knead 5 minutes or until dough becomes smooth and elastic. Place in a large bowl sprayed with cooking spray, turning once to coat top of dough. Cover and let rise in a warm place (80 to 85 degrees) 1 hour or until doubled in size. Turn dough onto a lightly floured surface and punch down. Shape dough into an 8 x 10-inch rectangle. Sprinkle ⅓ cup oats over dough. Starting with 1 long edge, roll up dough jelly-roll fashion. Place in a 5 x 9-inch loaf pan sprayed with cooking spray; spray top of dough. Sprinkle remaining 2 tablespoons oats over top of dough. Spray top of dough with cooking spray again. Cover and let rise in a warm place 1 hour or until doubled in size.

Preheat oven to 375 degrees. Bake 35 to 40 minutes or until bread is golden brown and sounds hollow when tapped. Serve warm.

Yield: 1 loaf bread

A pair of fine feathered friends has taken up residence on this Cardinal Wreath! Trimmed with greenery, bows, and a little birdhouse, it lends an air of natural charm to your holiday decor.

CRANBERRY-APPLE TURNOVERS

TURNOVERS

- 2½ cups peeled, cored, and chopped tart cooking apples (about 3 apples)
- ¾ cup fresh cranberries
- 1 cup granulated sugar
- ¼ cup chopped walnuts
- 2 tablespoons all-purpose flour
- ½ teaspoon ground cinnamon
- ¼ teaspoon ground nutmeg
- 2 sheets (one 17¼-ounce package) frozen puff pastry dough, thawed according to package directions

GLAZE

- ½ cup sifted confectioners sugar
- 2 teaspoons milk

For turnovers, combine apples, cranberries, sugar, walnuts, flour, cinnamon, and nutmeg in a large saucepan. Stirring occasionally, bring to a boil over medium heat. Reduce heat, cover, and simmer about 5 minutes or until apples are tender. Remove from heat.

Preheat oven to 400 degrees. On a lightly floured surface, cut each sheet of pastry into fourths. Spoon about ¼ cup apple mixture into center of each pastry square. Fold dough in half diagonally over filling to form a triangle; use a fork to crimp edges together. Place on a greased baking sheet. Bake 16 to 18 minutes or until golden brown.

For glaze, combine sugar and milk in a small bowl; stir until smooth. Drizzle glaze over warm turnovers. Serve warm or at room temperature.

Yield: 8 servings

TABLE RUNNER

For runner (pages 14 and 15), you will need fabric, fusible interfacing, and thread to match fabric.

1. Cut 2 pieces of fabric and 1 piece of interfacing ¼" larger on all sides than desired finished size of table runner.
2. Follow manufacturer's instructions to fuse interfacing to wrong side of 1 fabric piece.
3. Place fabric pieces right sides together. Leaving an opening for turning, use a ¼" seam allowance and sew fabric pieces together. Cut corners diagonally, turn right side out, and press. Sew final closure by hand.

RUSTIC NAPKIN RINGS

For each napkin ring (page 16 or 17), you will need one 1½" length cut from a cardboard paper towel tube, 5½" each of 1½"w and 2"w ribbon, small twigs, artificial berries, preserved boxwood greenery, jute twine, hot glue gun, and glue sticks.

1. Center and glue 2"w ribbon to outside of tube, overlapping ends. Fold edges of ribbon to inside of tube; glue in place. Glue 1½"w ribbon to inside of tube, overlapping ends.
2. For twig-covered napkin ring, glue 2 layers of 1½" long twigs around napkin ring, covering ribbon. Glue several boxwood leaves and berries to napkin ring.
3. For boxwood-trimmed napkin ring, glue boxwood along center of napkin ring. Tie jute around a small bundle of twigs; glue bundle to napkin ring. Glue berries to each side of bundle.

TWIG AND BERRY CANDLES

For each candle (page 15), you will need a pillar candle, 2"w ribbon, twigs, artificial berries on wired stems, preserved boxwood greenery, wire cutters, jute braid trim, hot glue gun, and glue sticks.

1. Measure around candle; add 1". Cut ribbon the determined measurement. Cut 3 lengths of jute trim 6" longer than ribbon. Cut twigs, berries, and boxwood same height as candle.
2. Glue ribbon around base of candle, overlapping ends. Glue twigs, berries, and boxwood to ribbon.
3. Knot lengths of jute trim together around base of candle.

CARDINAL WREATH

An outdoor winter scene comes to life on our merry wreath (page 18). We began by hot gluing preserved boxwood greenery and artificial berries to a purchased 16" dia. mossy wreath with a bark bow. A multi-loop bow made from wired ribbon was then glued to the wreath.

Next, we painted the porch and perch of a 4¾" high wooden birdhouse ornament red. We glued a small green wooden heart over the door and then sprayed the entire birdhouse lightly with Design Master® glossy wood tone spray (available at craft stores and florist shops). Accents of artificial snow were added to the rooftop and perch. A bundle of twigs glued inside the opening of the wreath forms a steady base on which to glue the birdhouse. A pair of pretty cardinals highlights this cozy winter scene.

"Dear Santa" Party

Writing letters to Santa is an exciting part of the season for youngsters — and it's even more fun to bring the letters to a special party and place them in Santa's mailbox for delivery! Along with the invitations, send packets of candy-striped stationery so parents can help children compose their wish lists before the party. The candy-striped decorating theme includes paper plates and napkins to coordinate with the mailbox centerpiece, and there's a candy-print tablecloth with a vinyl cover to sew. Santa pins and little mailboxes filled with treats make cute take-home favors. Sure to please, our menu features tried-and-true favorites for kids.

Christmas Tree Hamburgers

Candy Cane Gelatin Cutouts

Jolly Snowman Cookies

Snowball Cookies

Chocolate Yogurt Shakes

Kids will love these Christmas Tree Hamburgers! The buns are cut out with cookie cutters and trimmed with sweet pepper stars and garlands of squeeze cheese. Chocolate Yogurt Shakes are a delicious — and healthy — treat, and Candy Cane Gelatin Cutouts are striped with sweetened whipped cream. Purchased miniature mailboxes are personalized with paint pens and decorated with candy-striped fabric and colorful curling ribbon.

CHRISTMAS TREE HAMBURGERS

16 4½-inch hamburger buns
2 pounds lean ground beef
1 envelope (1.34 ounces) dry onion soup mix
   Sweet red pepper and canned American process cheese spread to garnish
   Bugle-shaped corn chips and desired vegetables, relishes, cheese, and condiments to serve

Use a 4-inch-high tree-shaped cookie cutter to cut out tree from top and bottom of each bun. Store tree-shaped buns in an airtight container until ready to serve.

In a medium bowl, combine ground beef and soup mix. Shape meat mixture into sixteen 4-inch-high triangular shapes. Cook in a large skillet over medium heat to desired doneness. Transfer to paper towels to drain. Cover and keep warm until ready to serve.

Use a star-shaped aspic cutter to cut out stars from red pepper. To serve, assemble hamburgers on plates; garnish with process cheese and red pepper stars. Serve with bugle-shaped corn chips and desired vegetables, relishes, cheese, and condiments.

Yield: 16 hamburgers

CHOCOLATE YOGURT SHAKES

2 cups chocolate milk
2 cups chocolate frozen yogurt, softened
2 cups crushed ice
½ cup chocolate syrup

In a blender, combine all ingredients; process until well blended. Serve immediately.

Yield: about eight 6-ounce servings

SNOWBALL COOKIES

2 cups sifted confectioners sugar
6 cups crisp rice cereal
1 cup raisins
1 cup chopped pecans
4 cups miniature marshmallows
¼ cup butter or margarine
1 teaspoon vanilla extract
½ teaspoon almond extract

Place confectioners sugar in a large bowl. In another large bowl, combine cereal, raisins, and pecans.

In a medium saucepan, combine marshmallows and butter. Stirring constantly, cook over medium heat until smooth. Remove from heat; stir in extracts. Pour marshmallow mixture over cereal mixture; stir until well coated. Using greased hands, shape mixture into 1½-inch balls. Coat with sugar. Store in an airtight container.

Yield: about 6½ dozen cookies

JOLLY SNOWMAN COOKIES

1 cup butter or margarine, softened
1½ cups granulated sugar
1 egg
1 teaspoon vanilla extract
2¾ cups all-purpose flour
¼ teaspoon salt
Pretzels
Miniature chocolate chips

Preheat oven to 350 degrees. In a medium bowl, cream butter and sugar until fluffy. Add egg and vanilla; beat until smooth. In a small bowl, combine flour and salt. Add dry ingredients to creamed mixture; stir until a soft dough forms. For each cookie, shape 3 small balls of dough, graduated in size. Place on a greased baking sheet and flatten balls slightly to resemble a snowman (cookies should be about 4½-inches

Sure to bring smiles to children's faces, Jolly Snowman Cookies are cleverly decorated with pretzels and chocolate chips. Snowball Cookies can be tucked into the little mailboxes for take-home treats. Santa Pins are fashioned from crafting foam and attached to candy canes with chenille stems.

long). Break pretzels into twig shapes. Insert pieces of broken pretzels into sides of cookies for arms. Press small pieces of pretzels onto cookies for mouths. Press chocolate chips onto cookies for eyes, noses, and buttons. Bake 10 to 12 minutes or until edges are light brown. Cool completely on a wire rack. Store in an airtight container.

Yield: about 14 cookies

CANDY CANE GELATIN CUTOUTS

2½ cups apple juice
2 boxes (6 ounces each) raspberry-flavored gelatin
¼ cup water
2 tablespoons granulated sugar
1 envelope unflavored gelatin
¼ cup whipping cream

In a medium saucepan, bring apple juice to a boil. Remove from heat, add raspberry-flavored gelatin, and stir until gelatin dissolves. Pour gelatin mixture

into a 9 x 13-inch baking pan. Cover and refrigerate 1 hour or until very firm. Dip bottom of pan in hot water for 10 to 15 seconds to loosen gelatin. Use a 3½-inch-high candy cane-shaped cookie cutter to cut out shapes. Use a spatula to transfer candy canes to individual plates.

Place a small bowl and beaters from an electric mixer in freezer. In a small saucepan, combine water, sugar, and unflavored gelatin. Let stand 1 minute. Cook over low heat, stirring until gelatin and sugar dissolve. Remove from heat. In chilled bowl, beat whipping cream until soft peaks form. Add sugar mixture and beat until stiff peaks form. Transfer topping to a pastry bag fitted with a small star tip and pipe stripes on candy canes. Loosely cover and refrigerate until ready to serve.

Yield: about 12 servings

Before the party, you'll want to hand deliver a colorful "Dear Santa" Party Packet to each child. The packet includes a mailbox-shaped invitation, stenciled stationery, and an envelope addressed to Santa Claus.

TABLECLOTH WITH VINYL COVER

For tablecloth (page 20), you will need fabric (see Step 1 for amount) and thread to match fabric.

For vinyl cover (page 20), you will need clear medium weight (8-gauge) vinyl (available at fabric stores; see Step 1 for amount), fabric for binding (see Step 2 for amount), thread to match binding fabric, and tracing paper.

TABLECLOTH

1. Determine desired size of tablecloth. Cut a piece of fabric ½″ larger on all sides than determined size.
2. Press edges of fabric ¼″ to wrong side; press ¼″ to wrong side again and stitch in place.

VINYL COVER

1. Cut a piece of vinyl 3″ smaller on all sides than tablecloth.

2. For binding, measure around edges of vinyl; add 1″. Cut a 2″w bias strip of fabric the determined measurement (pieced as necessary). Matching wrong sides, press bias strip in half lengthwise; unfold. Press long raw edges to center; refold binding. Unfold 1 end of binding and press ½″ to wrong side; refold binding.
3. (*Note:* To sew vinyl, use tracing paper on both sides of seam to prevent presser foot from dragging; tear away paper after sewing.) Beginning with unpressed end of binding, insert edge of vinyl into fold of binding. Stitching close to inner edge of binding, sew binding to vinyl, mitering binding at corners.

SANTA'S MAILBOX

For mailbox (page 21), you will need a standard size mailbox, white spray paint, 1½″w red and ¾″w green plastic tape (available at hardware stores), 1″ high lettering stencil, removable tape (optional), stencil brush, paper towels, green acrylic paint, red paint pen, foam brush, screwdriver (to remove flag holder and latch parts), and craft knife.

1. Remove flag holder, flag, and latch parts from mailbox. Spray paint mailbox white; use foam brush to paint flag holder and latch parts (including screws) green. Allow to dry.
2. For address, use green paint and lettering stencil and follow Step 2 of Stenciling, page 123, to stencil the following words on 1 side of mailbox: SANTA CLAUS, 8 REINDEER LN, NORTH POLE.
3. For border around address, apply pieces of green tape to mailbox ½″ from address.
4. For wide stripes, apply red tape pieces to mailbox, beginning at bottom edge on front of box and spacing pieces 1½″ apart. Use craft knife to trim pieces to fit around address border.
5. For narrow stripes, use paint pen and a ruler to paint 2 lines ¼″ apart between each pair of wide stripes.
6. Reattach flag, flag holder, and latch parts to mailbox.

"DEAR SANTA" PARTY PACKETS

For each invitation and stationery set (this page), you will need red, green, and white cover stock paper; a 4¾″ x 6½″ envelope; acetate for stencils (available at craft or art supply stores); craft knife; cutting mat or a thick layer of newspapers; removable tape (optional); stencil brushes; paper towels; red and green acrylic paint; red permanent felt-tip pen with fine point; one $\frac{3}{8}$″ dia. white button; red thread; needle; craft glue; and tracing paper. *For each stationery pocket (page 24),* you will need two 9″ x 16″ pieces of desired fabric, a 7$\frac{1}{4}$″ x 10$\frac{1}{4}$″ piece of clear medium weight (8-gauge) vinyl (available at fabric stores), a 2″w x 1$\frac{3}{8}$ yds long bias strip for binding, thread to match binding fabric, paper-backed fusible web, tracing paper, one $\frac{1}{2}$″ dia. Velcro® brand hook and loop fastener, and Velcro® brand adhesive.

INVITATION
1. Cut a 7″ x 10″ piece of white paper. Matching short edges, fold paper in half.
2. Using mailbox pattern, page 115, follow Stenciling, page 123, to stencil mailbox on paper with top of mailbox along fold of paper.
3. For narrow stripes, use red pen and a ruler to draw 2 lines $\frac{1}{8}$″ apart between each pair of red stripes.
4. Cutting just outside stenciled design, cut out invitation.
5. Trace flag pattern, page 115, onto tracing paper; cut out. Use pattern to cut flag from red paper. Sew button and flag to front of invitation.
6. Cut a 1$\frac{3}{8}$″ x 2$\frac{3}{4}$″ piece from green paper and a 1$\frac{1}{8}$″ x 2$\frac{1}{2}$″ piece from white paper. Use red pen to write ''Dear Santa Party'' on white paper. Glue white paper to center of green paper; glue green paper to mailbox.

STATIONERY SET
1. Cut a 6$\frac{1}{4}$″ x 9″ piece of white paper.
2. For wide red stripes, use stripes pattern, page 115, and follow

Stenciling, page 123, to stencil stripes along 1 short edge (top) of paper.
3. For narrow stripes, use red pen to draw 2 straight lines $\frac{1}{8}$″ apart between each pair of wide red stripes.
4. Cut a $\frac{1}{4}$″ x 6$\frac{1}{4}$″ strip from green paper; glue strip $\frac{1}{8}$″ below red stripes.
5. Use pen to write ''Dear Santa'' on stationery and ''Santa Claus, 8 Reindeer Lane, North Pole'' on front of envelope.

STATIONERY POCKET
1. Cut a piece of web same size as 1 fabric piece. Follow web manufacturer's instructions to fuse wrong sides of fabric pieces together.
2. Use pocket pattern, page 114, and follow Tracing Patterns, page 123, extending bottom of pattern 10″; cut out. Use pattern to cut pocket from fused fabric.
3. For binding, match wrong sides and press bias strip in half lengthwise; unfold. Press long raw edges to center; refold binding.
4. (*Note:* To sew vinyl, use tracing paper on both sides of seam to prevent presser foot from dragging; tear away paper after sewing.) To bind 1 short edge (top) of vinyl for pocket opening, cut a 7$\frac{1}{4}$″ length from binding. Insert edge of vinyl into fold of binding. Stitching close to inner edge of binding, sew binding to vinyl.
5. Unfold 1 end of remaining binding and press $\frac{1}{2}$″ to wrong side; refold binding. Matching side and bottom edges of vinyl to square end of pocket fabric piece, place vinyl piece on pocket fabric piece. Beginning with unpressed end of binding, insert edges of fabric and vinyl into fold of binding. Stitching close to inner edge of binding, sew binding to pocket, mitering binding at corners.

6. Being careful not to touch vinyl with iron, press flap 3″ toward pocket.
7. Glue 1 side of Velcro® fastener to inside of flap. Making sure circles will meet, glue remaining side of fastener to front of pocket.
8. Place 1 invitation and 1 stationery set in pocket.

SANTA PINS

For each pin (page 23), you will need white, pink, peach, and red $\frac{1}{16}$″ thick crafting foam; black dimensional paint in a squeeze bottle; craft glue; tracing paper; 1 pin back; small sharp scissors or craft knife (for cutting foam); and hole punch.

1. Trace Santa pattern, page 114, onto tracing paper; cut out. Use a pencil to draw around outer edge of pattern on peach foam; cut out.
2. Cut hat portion from pattern. Draw around hat pattern on red foam; cut out. Draw around beard pattern on white foam; cut out.
3. Use hole punch to cut 1 circle each from white, pink, and red foam. Cut pink circle in half.
4. Matching edges, glue hat to top of peach shape; glue beard to bottom of shape. Glue white circle to hat for pom-pom; glue red circle and pink half circles to face for nose and cheeks. Use paint to paint eyes. Allow glue and paint to dry.
5. Glue pin back to back of Santa. Allow to dry.

WINTRY ELEGANCE

Inspired by the icy splendor of a winter landscape, this dinner setting glitters with decorations of silver and white. Handcrafted topiaries and twig trees are attractively arranged with glowing votive candles on a table laid with your finest crystal and silver. Handsome bows decorate the handwritten menu cards and stenciled place mats, and frosty snowflakes top little place card favor boxes filled with confections. Making up a menu worthy of this impressive table setting, our elegant dishes promise to make the evening a sparkling success.

Cranberry-Brie in Pastry

Hearts of Palm and Shrimp Salad

Châteaubriand with Caper Sauce

Sugar Snaps with Buttered Pecans

Potato Gratiné

Bananas Foster Crêpes

Ginger Champagne

A tart-sweet cranberry topping lends holiday color to Cranberry-Brie in Pastry. The flavorful appetizers are easy to make with sheets of purchased phyllo pastry.

CRANBERRY-BRIE IN PASTRY

2 teaspoons vegetable oil
¼ cup finely chopped onion
¼ cup finely chopped celery
1 can (16 ounces) whole berry cranberry sauce
2 tablespoons sour cream
1 teaspoon balsamic vinegar
4 sheets frozen phyllo pastry, thawed according to package directions
  Vegetable cooking spray
1 package (4½ ounces) Brie cheese, cut into 18 small pieces

In a small saucepan, heat oil over medium heat. Add onion and celery; cook until tender. Stir in cranberry sauce, sour cream, and vinegar. Stirring occasionally, bring to a boil over medium heat and cook 15 minutes or until thickened. Remove from heat; set aside.

Preheat oven to 375 degrees. Spray each sheet of phyllo pastry with cooking spray. Stack pastry sheets on top of each other; cut into eighteen 3-inch squares. Press 1 pastry square into each tin of a greased miniature muffin pan. Place 1 piece cheese in center of each pastry square. Spoon a heaping teaspoonful cranberry mixture over top of each piece of cheese. Bake 12 to 15 minutes or until golden brown. Serve warm.

Yield: 1½ dozen appetizers

GINGER CHAMPAGNE

¼ cup light corn syrup
¼ cup granulated sugar
2 tablespoons minced crystallized ginger
½ cup vodka
3 bottles (750 ml each) champagne, chilled

In a small saucepan, combine corn syrup, sugar, and ginger. Stirring occasionally, bring to a boil over medium heat; reduce heat to medium-low and simmer 2 minutes. Remove from heat; stir in vodka. Cover and refrigerate 8 hours or overnight. Strain sugar mixture and discard ginger.

Place sugar mixture into a 3-quart container. Slowly pour champagne into sugar mixture. Serve immediately.

Yield: about nineteen 4-ounce servings

SUGAR SNAPS WITH BUTTERED PECANS

¼ cup butter or margarine
½ cup chopped pecans
3 boxes (8 ounces each) frozen sugar snap peas, thawed
  Salt
  Ground black pepper

In a medium skillet, melt butter over medium heat. Stirring occasionally, add pecans and cook until pecans are slightly darker in color. Stir in peas and cook until heated through. Salt and pepper to taste. Serve hot.

Yield: about 10 servings

CHÂTEAUBRIAND WITH CAPER SAUCE

3½ pounds châteaubriand,
    trimmed of fat
    Olive oil, salt, and ground black
    pepper
2 teaspoons garlic powder
10 to 12 slices bacon
1 cup water
¼ cup butter or margarine
2 large onions, chopped
3 tablespoons all-purpose flour
1 teaspoon balsamic vinegar
1 teaspoon dried tarragon leaves
¾ cup whipping cream
½ cup dry white wine, divided
1 bottle (3½ ounces) capers,
    undrained

Fresh tarragon to garnish

Preheat oven to 400 degrees. Rub beef with oil. Sprinkle salt, pepper, and garlic powder over beef. Wrap bacon around beef, securing with toothpicks. Place beef in a greased 9 x 13-inch baking pan; pour water into pan. Insert a meat thermometer into center of meat. Place in oven, reduce temperature to 350 degrees, and bake 35 to 40 minutes or until thermometer registers 150 degrees (medium-rare).

For sauce, melt butter in a large skillet over medium heat. Add onions; cook until tender. Stirring constantly, add flour, vinegar, and dried tarragon; cook 3 minutes. Gradually stir in cream and ¼ cup wine; bring to a boil. Stirring constantly, boil 5 minutes or until thickened. Remove from heat; stir in capers and remaining ¼ cup wine.

To serve, cut meat into about 1½-inch-thick slices. Remove toothpicks. Spoon sauce over meat and garnish with fresh tarragon.

Yield: about 10 servings

HEARTS OF PALM AND SHRIMP SALAD

½ cup olive oil
¼ cup red wine vinegar
¼ cup water
1 tablespoon granulated sugar
2 teaspoons lemon juice
1 teaspoon Dijon-style mustard
1 teaspoon Worcestershire sauce
¾ teaspoon garlic salt
¼ teaspoon ground black pepper
3 cans (14 ounces each) hearts of
    palm, drained
1½ pounds large shrimp, cooked,
    peeled, and deveined
6 slices bacon, cooked, drained,
    and crumbled

Red cabbage leaves to serve
Fresh parsley to garnish

In a small bowl, whisk first 9 ingredients until well blended. If desired, cut hearts of palm in half lengthwise. Place hearts of palm, shrimp, and bacon in a 1-gallon resealable plastic bag; pour dressing over. Seal bag and refrigerate 8 hours or overnight to allow flavors to blend.

Reserve dressing. To serve, arrange hearts of palm and shrimp on cabbage leaves on individual serving plates. Pour reserved dressing over each salad. Garnish with parsley.

Yield: about 10 servings

Rich Hearts of Palm and Shrimp Salad is marinated in a tangy dressing and artfully arranged on red cabbage leaves.

29

Roasted to perfection, tender Châteaubriand is served with a creamy Caper Sauce. Sugar Snaps with Buttered Pecans and Potato Gratiné complement the elegant entrée.

POTATO GRATINÉ

2 large russet potatoes, peeled and
    cut into ¼-inch-thick slices
1½ cups (6 ounces) shredded
    Cheddar cheese
¾ cup whipping cream
¾ cup dry white wine
4 eggs
1 teaspoon salt
½ teaspoon ground white pepper
½ teaspoon garlic powder

Place potato slices in a large saucepan and cover with water. Bring to a boil and cook until potatoes are tender; drain.

Preheat oven to 350 degrees. Press aluminum foil around bottoms of 8 greased 4-inch tart pans with removable bottoms. Arrange potato slices in pans. Sprinkle cheese evenly over potatoes. In a medium bowl, whisk

cream, wine, eggs, salt, pepper, and garlic powder. Pour cream mixture evenly over potatoes. Bake 25 to 30 minutes or until golden brown. To serve, remove from pans and place on individual plates.

Yield: 8 servings

Served warm with scoops of vanilla ice cream, sweet Bananas Foster Crêpes are spiced with cinnamon and enhanced with banana liqueur and rum.

BANANAS FOSTER CRÊPES

CRÊPES
- ¾ cup milk
- ½ cup all-purpose flour
- 1 egg
- 1 tablespoon granulated sugar
- 2 teaspoons vegetable oil
- ⅛ teaspoon salt

FILLING
- 4 ripe bananas
  Lemon juice
- ⅔ cup firmly packed brown sugar
- 6 tablespoons butter or margarine
- ½ teaspoon ground cinnamon
- ¼ cup banana liqueur
- ¼ cup rum

  Vanilla ice cream to serve

For crêpes, combine all ingredients in a medium bowl; beat until smooth. Heat a lightly greased 8-inch skillet over medium heat. Spoon about 2 tablespoons batter into skillet. Tilt skillet to spread batter evenly in bottom of pan to form a 5½-inch circle. Cook until edges are light brown; remove from skillet. Repeat with remaining batter. Separate crêpes with waxed paper. (If making in advance, cover and refrigerate; bring to room temperature before serving.)

For filling, peel bananas. Cut each banana in half crosswise and in half again lengthwise. Brush with lemon juice. In a large skillet, combine sugar, butter, and cinnamon. Stirring constantly, cook over medium heat until sugar dissolves. Add bananas; cook 3 to 4 minutes, turning once. Pour liqueur and rum over bananas and cook 2 minutes longer. Remove from heat. Reserving sauce, place 2 banana slices on each crêpe. Fold edges of crêpe over bananas; place on serving plate. Spoon reserved sauce over crêpes. Serve immediately with ice cream.

Yield: 8 servings

Light, sparkling Ginger Champagne makes a refreshing cocktail. Handwritten Menu Cards provide an attractive preview of the evening's fare, and Snowflake Favor Boxes filled with purchased candies double as place cards. The Elegant Place Mats are stenciled with a silvery bow.

ELEGANT PLACE MATS

For each place mat (this page), you will need a purchased white fabric place mat, acetate for stencil (available at craft stores), permanent felt-tip pen with fine point, craft knife, cutting mat or thick layer of newspapers, removable tape (optional), paper towels, metallic silver fabric paint, stencil brush, and iridescent glitter.

Using bow pattern, page 118, and fabric paint, follow Stenciling, page 123, to stencil bow design at center top of place mat; before paint dries, sprinkle glitter over wet paint. Allow to dry; shake off excess glitter.

MENU CARDS

For each menu card (this page), you will need a 7½" x 9½" piece of green vinyl cover stock (available at photocopy shops), a 6¾" x 8¾" piece of silver foil wrapping paper, a 6" x 8" piece of heavy white paper, ½ yd of ¼" dia. silver twisted cord, tracing paper, graphite transfer paper, black pen with fine point, spray adhesive, hot glue gun, and glue sticks.

1. Trace "Menu" pattern, page 118, onto tracing paper. Use transfer paper to transfer design to top of heavy white paper. Use pen to draw over transferred lines and to write remainder of menu.
2. Use spray adhesive to glue wrapping paper to cover stock; glue menu to wrapping paper.
3. Tie cord into a bow and knot each end; hot glue bow to menu card.

SNOWFLAKE FAVOR BOXES

For each box (page 32), you will need a 4" dia. Shaker box, metallic silver spray paint, a 5" square each of white satin fabric and polyester bonded batting, fabric marking pencil, 14" each of 5/8"w white grosgrain ribbon and 3/8"w silver braid trim, 1 yd of 1/16" dia. silver cord, a 4" dia. purchased snowflake ornament, a 1½" x 3" piece of heavy white paper, black pen with fine point, hole punch, and craft glue.

1. Spray paint inside and outside of box and lid. Allow to dry.
2. Use lid as a pattern to cut 1 circle from batting. Use fabric marking pencil to draw around lid on wrong side of fabric. Cut out fabric ½" outside pencil line. Clip fabric at ½" intervals to within ⅛" of pencil line.
3. To cover lid, glue batting to lid. Center fabric circle right side up over batting. Alternating sides and pulling fabric taut, glue clipped edges of fabric to side of lid. Allow to dry.
4. To cover side of lid, glue ribbon around side of lid; center and glue braid trim to ribbon. Allow to dry.
5. Glue snowflake to lid; allow to dry.
6. Place favor in box. Place lid on box.
7. For tag, punch a hole in 1 corner of white paper. Use pen to write name on tag. Tie cord around box; thread tag onto 1 end of cord. Tie cord into a bow and knot each end.

TOPIARY TREES

For trees (pages 26 and 27), you will need clay pots; floral foam; matte white spray paint; silver trim, wired ribbon, and cord; silk ivy; sheet moss; purchased white twigs covered with glitter; metallic silver acrylic paint; iridescent glitter; small sponge pieces;

wire cutters; hot glue gun; and glue sticks.

For rose and poinsettia tree, you will also need a 6" dia. topiary form with base, white silk roses, and large and small silver silk poinsettias.

For poinsettia tree, you will also need a 4" dia. plastic foam ball and two 9" dia. silver silk poinsettias.

For moss tree, you will also need a 9"h x 4" dia. plastic foam cone, white silk roses, and Design Master® moss green spray paint (available at craft stores and florist shops).

ROSE AND POINSETTIA TREE

1. Spray paint pot and trunk of topiary form white; allow to dry.
2. Glue form into pot. If necessary, place smaller pieces of foam into pot to stabilize tree.
3. Glue moss over foam in pot, covering foam completely.
4. Insert several twigs into foam around tree trunk.
5. Trim rose, ivy, and poinsettia stems to 2". Insert stems into foam ball, covering ball completely. If necessary, glue leaves to foam ball to fill spaces.
6. Glue trim around pot below rim.
7. Tie a length of ribbon into a bow. Glue bow to base of trunk.

POINSETTIA TREE

1. Spray paint pot white; allow to dry.
2. Use a damp sponge piece to lightly stamp desired areas of pot with metallic paint. Sprinkle glitter over wet paint. Allow to dry; shake off excess glitter.
3. Glue floral foam into pot to within ½" of rim. Glue moss over foam in pot, covering foam completely.
4. For trunk, insert two or more 9½" twigs 2" into foam ball. Insert trunk 2" into foam in pot.

5. Trim ivy and poinsettia stems to 2". Insert 1 poinsettia stem into front and 1 into back of foam ball, overlapping petals slightly. Insert sprig of ivy into moss at base of trunk.

MOSS TREE

1. Spray paint pot white; allow to dry.
2. Glue floral foam into pot to within ½" of rim. Glue moss over foam in pot, covering foam completely.
3. For trunk, insert two or more 6" twigs 2" into bottom of cone. Insert trunk 2" into foam in pot.
4. Lightly spray pieces of moss with moss green paint; allow to dry. Glue moss to sides and bottom of cone, covering cone completely; allow to dry.
5. Trim rose and ivy stems to 2". Insert stems of roses and ivy into tree.
6. Tie two lengths of ribbon into bows; glue to top of tree.
7. Glue trim around pot below rim. Tie cord into a bow and knot each end; glue bow to trim.

TWIG TREES

1. To prepare pot, follow Steps 1 - 3 of Poinsettia Tree instructions.
2. Insert several twigs into center of foam to form tree shape.

Teen Scene

Merriment will abound when the gang gets together for this party! They'll have lots of fun making delicious Christmas cookie "cards" for all their friends and crafting envelopes to deliver them. Featuring holiday cutouts, the cookies are baked ahead of time and then decorated with melted candies during the party. You'll also provide sponge-painting kits that include everything needed to make the patterned paper for the envelopes (the paper's great for wrapping gifts, too!). With all the festive activity, teens are sure to work up an appetite — so you'll want to have our tempting assortment of munchies on hand.

Almond Caramel Corn

Onion-Bacon Dip

Festive Cheese Ball

Chocolate Brownies

Frozen Peppermint Dessert

Christmas Card Cookies

Hungry teens will gobble up Almond Caramel Corn! The crunchy snack is packed with almonds and lightly sweetened with brown sugar and molasses. Zesty Onion-Bacon Dip is great with fresh veggies or chips.

ALMOND CARAMEL CORN

     2 cups whole unsalted almonds
       Vegetable cooking spray
    16 cups popped popcorn
     1 cup firmly packed brown sugar
     2 tablespoons light corn syrup
     2 tablespoons molasses
     1 teaspoon almond extract
     ½ teaspoon salt
     ½ teaspoon baking soda

Preheat oven to 350 degrees. To toast almonds, place almonds on an ungreased baking sheet. Stirring occasionally, bake 8 to 10 minutes or until almonds are slightly darker in color. Cool completely on baking sheet.

Spray inside of a 14 x 20-inch oven cooking bag with cooking spray. Place popcorn and almonds in bag. In a 2-quart microwave-safe bowl, combine next 3 ingredients. Microwave on high power (100%) 2 minutes or until mixture boils. Stir and microwave 2 minutes longer. Stir in remaining ingredients. Pour syrup over popcorn mixture; stir and shake until well coated. Microwave 1½ minutes. Stir, shake, and microwave 1½ minutes longer. Spread on aluminum foil sprayed with cooking spray. Cool completely. Store in an airtight container.

Yield: about 18 cups caramel corn

ONION-BACON DIP

     2 cups sour cream
     2 cups mayonnaise
     1 envelope (1 ounce) dry
       onion soup mix
    1½ teaspoons garlic powder
     1 jar (2 ounces) real bacon pieces
       Fresh parsley to garnish
       Fresh vegetables or chips to serve

In a medium bowl, combine first 4 ingredients; stir until well blended. Reserving 1 tablespoon bacon, stir in remaining bacon. Cover and refrigerate 8 hours or overnight. Garnish with reserved bacon and parsley. Serve with fresh vegetables or chips.

Yield: about 4 cups dip

FROZEN PEPPERMINT DESSERT

½ gallon vanilla-flavored frozen
    yogurt or ice cream, softened
½ cup crushed peppermint candies
    Purchased red decorating icing,
    candy canes, and round green
    and white mint candies to
    decorate

In a large bowl, combine yogurt and crushed candy. Spoon into an 11 x 15-inch tree-shaped pan. Cover and freeze until firm. To remove from pan, dip bottom of pan in hot water; invert onto a serving plate. Arrange candy canes and green and white candies on top of dessert. Transfer icing into a pastry bag fitted with a small petal tip. Pipe icing for bows. Cover and store in freezer until ready to serve.

Yield: about 18 servings

CHOCOLATE BROWNIES

½ cup butter or margarine, softened
1 cup granulated sugar
4 eggs
1½ cups chocolate-flavored syrup
1 teaspoon vanilla extract
18 chocolate wafer cookies, finely
    ground
½ cup all-purpose flour
1 package (6 ounces) semisweet
    chocolate chips

Preheat oven to 350 degrees. In a medium bowl, cream butter and sugar until fluffy. Beat in next 3 ingredients. Add cookie crumbs and flour; mix until well blended. Stir in chocolate chips. Pour into a greased and floured 9 x 13-inch baking pan. Bake 40 to 45 minutes or until dry on top and set in center. Cool in pan. Cut into squares. Store in an airtight container.

Yield: about 1½ dozen brownies

Molded in a tree shape, Frozen Peppermint Dessert is a cool combination of frozen vanilla yogurt and crushed peppermint candies. It's perfect paired with super-moist Chocolate Brownies.

This Festive Cheese Ball, a tasty blend of cheeses with crisp bits of celery and carrots, is decorated to resemble a Christmas ball ornament.

FESTIVE CHEESE BALL

1 package (8 ounces) Neufchâtel
   cheese, softened
½ cup finely chopped celery
⅓ cup grated Parmesan cheese
¼ cup shredded carrot
2 tablespoons mayonnaise
2 tablespoons dried minced onion
   Sweet red and yellow peppers
     and green onions to garnish
   Crackers to serve

In a medium bowl, combine first 6 ingredients. On a serving plate, shape cheese mixture into a 1-inch-high by 5-inch-diameter circle. Cover and refrigerate 8 hours or overnight to allow flavors to blend.

Garnish cheese ball with peppers and tops of green onions. To serve, let stand at room temperature 20 to 30 minutes or until softened. Serve with crackers.

Yield: 1 cheese ball

CHRISTMAS CARD COOKIES

1 cup butter or margarine, softened
1 cup granulated sugar
2 eggs
1 teaspoon vanilla extract
3⅓ cups all-purpose flour
1 teaspoon baking powder
½ teaspoon salt
   Vegetable cooking spray

2 cups hard candies (we used
   40 candies each of red
   and green)
  Red and green paste food coloring
   and ribbon to decorate

Trace cookie patterns, page 39, onto tracing paper; cut out. In a large bowl, cream butter and sugar until fluffy. Add eggs and vanilla; beat until smooth. In a medium bowl, combine flour, baking powder, and salt. Add dry ingredients to creamed mixture; stir until a soft dough forms. Cover and refrigerate 1 hour.

Preheat oven to 350 degrees. Line baking sheets with aluminum foil; spray foil with cooking spray. On a lightly floured surface, use a floured rolling pin to roll out dough to ¼-inch thickness. Using a sharp knife, cut dough into 4 x 5-inch rectangles. Transfer cookies to prepared baking sheets, leaving 1 inch between cookies. For each reindeer cookie, place reindeer and moon patterns on cookie and cut out shapes. For each star cookie, cut a 2½ x 3-inch rectangle from center of cookie; remove rectangle. Place star pattern on small rectangle and cut out shape. Place star in center of cookie. For each holly cookie, place holly pattern on cookie and cut out shape. Use knife to cut 3 holes for berries at 1 end of holly. For each cookie, use a drinking straw to make 2 holes ½ inch apart at top or one side edge for ribbon. Bake 12 to 14 minutes or until cookies are firm. Cool completely on foil.

In separate small saucepans, melt each color candy over medium heat. Spoon desired color of melted candy into each cutout shape in cookies. Allow candy to harden. Use a small paintbrush to paint food coloring on

tar cookies for stitches. Carefully
emove cookies from foil. Thread
ibbon through holes in cookies and tie
s desired. Store in an airtight
ontainer.
ield: about 1½ dozen cookies

OOKIE ENVELOPES

or each envelope (page 35), you will
eed Painted Paper (this page), red or
reen foil wrapping paper, white paper,
pray adhesive, craft glue, ½ yd each
f ⅛″w red and 1/16″w green satin
ibbon, poster board, pinking shears,
ole punch, and a Christmas Card
ookie (page 38).

. (*Note:* Use spray adhesive for all
luing unless otherwise indicated.) With
vrong sides together, glue foil wrapping
aper to painted paper. Use pinking
hears to cut a 6″ x 14½″ piece of
aper.
. For envelope, fold 1 short edge
bottom) of paper 6″ to foil side. Use
raft glue to glue side edges together to
orm envelope; allow to dry. For flap,
old remaining short edge (top) of paper
½″ to foil side.
. Punch 2 holes through envelope 1″
part, ½″ from center top of envelope.
lace cookie in envelope. Thread
ibbons through holes and tie into a
ow.
. For tag, glue a 4″ square of poster
oard to wrong side of foil wrapping
aper; trim wrapping paper even with
oster board. Cut desired shape from
ainted paper. Glue shape to foil side of
quare. For name box, cut a ½″ x 1½″
iece of white paper and glue to shape.
rim foil square to ⅛″ larger than
hape.

PAINTING KITS

For each kit (page 34), you will need a
white plastic mini basket, red Mylar®
gift paper, white tissue paper, Miracle
Sponges™ (dry compressed sponges
available at craft stores), bottles of red
and green acrylic paint, permanent felt-
tip pen with fine point, tracing paper,
red and green paper, 7″ each of ⅛″w
red and 1/16″w green satin ribbon,
¼″w red and ¼″w green grosgrain
ribbon, sprig of artificial holly, pinking
shears, hole punch, craft glue, and
Painted Paper (this page).

1. For basket, weave grosgrain ribbons
through basket and tie into a bow at
front of basket. Insert stem of holly sprig
behind bow. Line basket with gift paper
and tissue paper.
2. For sponge patterns, trace patterns,
page 120, onto tracing paper; cut out.
Use tracing paper patterns to cut
patterns from red and green paper.
3. For pattern envelope, use pinking
shears to cut a 3″ x 6″ piece of painted
paper. Fold 1 short edge (bottom) of
paper 2½″ to wrong side. Glue side
edges together to form envelope; allow
to dry. For flap, fold remaining short
edge (top) of paper 1″ to wrong side.
4. Punch hole close to 1 edge of each
red or green pattern and in 1 top corner
of envelope. Use lengths of satin ribbon
to tie patterns to envelope.
5. Place patterns and envelope, paint
bottles, sponges, and pen into basket.

PAINTED PAPER

For paper (page 35), you will need
white paper, plastic or coated paper
plates, and paper towels.
You will also need either a Painting Kit
(this page) *or* the following items:
Miracle Sponges™ (dry compressed
sponges available at craft stores), tracing
paper, permanent felt-tip pen with fine
point, and red and green acrylic paint.

1. (*Note:* If using Painting Kit, begin
with Step 2.) Trace patterns, page 120,
onto tracing paper and cut out.
2. For sponge shapes, use pen to draw
around patterns on sponges; cut out.
3. To paint with sponge shape, dampen
sponge. Pour paint on plate. Dip
sponge in paint; do not saturate. Dab
sponge on paper towels to remove
excess paint. Keeping sponge level,
place sponge on white paper. Lightly
press sponge with palm of hand;
carefully lift sponge. Dipping sponge in
paint as necessary, repeat as desired.
Allow to dry.

A Splendid Twelfth Night

Held on January 6 to celebrate Epiphany (the Wise Men's visit to Bethlehem), this magnificent party is a splendid way to wrap up the holiday season. Sumptuous trimmings of red, purple, and gold create a regal atmosphere. Tassels and gold mesh bows adorn the corners of a royal purple table topper stenciled with golden stars. Highlighted with gold and purple paint, clear glass plates become elegant serving dishes. A tasteful selection of hors d'oeuvres adds the crowning touch.

Macadamia Cheese Puffs

Marinated Mozzarella

Crab-Cream Cheese Bake

Cheesy Snack Mix

Orange Glazed Pecans

Hot Bacon-Cheese Dip

Imperial Champagne Cocktails

MACADAMIA CHEESE PUFFS

1 cup buttermilk biscuit mix
1 cup finely chopped unsalted
    macadamia nuts
1 cup (4 ounces) shredded Gruyère
    cheese
½ cup butter or margarine, softened
1 egg, beaten
½ teaspoon ground white pepper

Preheat oven to 375 degrees. In a
medium bowl, combine all ingredients;
stir until a soft dough forms. Drop
teaspoonfuls of dough onto a greased
baking sheet. Bake 12 to 15 minutes or
until edges are light brown. Cool on pan
2 minutes. Transfer to a wire rack to
cool completely. Store in an airtight
container.

Yield: about 6 dozen cheese puffs

MARINATED MOZZARELLA

1 pound mozzarella cheese, cut
    into thin 2-inch squares
¼ cup olive oil
2 tablespoons finely chopped fresh
    parsley
1 teaspoon garlic powder
1 teaspoon onion powder
1 teaspoon dried oregano leaves,
    crushed
¼ teaspoon ground black pepper
    Fresh basil to garnish
    Bagel chips or crackers to serve

Place cheese in a single layer in a
10 x 15-inch jellyroll pan. In a small
bowl, whisk next 6 ingredients. Pour
oil mixture over cheese. Cover and
refrigerate 8 hours or overnight to allow
flavors to blend, turning slices
occasionally. Arrange on a serving
plate; garnish with fresh basil. Serve
with bagel chips or crackers.

Yield: about 3 dozen cheese squares

*Delicious with bagel chips or crackers, slices of Marinated Mozzarella
get their mellow flavor from a mixture of herbs and olive oil. Shown on
previous page: Guests will love the buttery Macadamia Cheese Puffs.*

CRAB-CREAM CHEESE BAKE

1 package (8 ounces) cream cheese, softened
¼ cup chopped green onions
½ teaspoon dried dill weed
1 can (8 ounces) refrigerated crescent dinner rolls
1 can (6½ ounces) crabmeat, drained
1 egg yolk, beaten

Preheat oven to 350 degrees. In a medium bowl, combine cream cheese, onions, and dill weed. Unroll crescent roll dough onto a greased baking sheet, being careful not to separate dough into pieces. Press dough into an 8 x 11-inch rectangle. Spoon crabmeat lengthwise along center of dough. Spoon cream cheese mixture over crabmeat. Fold long edges of dough over cream cheese mixture, slightly overlapping edges; pinch edges together to seal. Place seam side down on baking sheet. Lightly brush top of dough with egg yolk. Cut slits in top of dough. Bake 20 to 22 minutes or until golden brown and flaky. Cut into 1-inch slices and serve warm.

Yield: about 12 servings

CHEESY SNACK MIX

14 cups (about 20 ounces) small pretzels
1 cup butter or margarine
1 cup grated Parmesan cheese
3 packages (1.25 ounces each) cheese sauce mix
2 packages (1 ounce each) ranch-style salad dressing mix
1 teaspoon garlic powder

Preheat oven to 350 degrees. Place pretzels in a large bowl. In a medium saucepan, melt butter over medium

The savory Crab-Cream Cheese Bake is encased in flaky pastry. Orange Glazed Pecans and Cheesy Snack Mix are perfect for nibbling.

heat. Remove from heat; stir in remaining ingredients. Pour over pretzels; stir until well coated. Transfer to 2 ungreased baking sheets. Bake 10 to 12 minutes or until golden brown. Cool completely on baking sheets. Store in an airtight container.

Yield: about 15½ cups snack mix

ORANGE GLAZED PECANS

½ cup granulated sugar
½ cup firmly packed brown sugar
½ cup sour cream
2 tablespoons frozen orange juice concentrate, thawed
1 teaspoon orange extract
3 cups unsalted pecan halves, toasted

Preheat oven to 350 degrees. In a medium saucepan, combine sugars, sour cream, and orange juice. Stirring

constantly, cook over medium-low heat until sugars dissolve. Using a pastry brush dipped in hot water, wash down any sugar crystals on sides of pan. Attach candy thermometer to pan, making sure thermometer does not touch bottom of pan. Increase heat to medium and bring to a boil. Cook, without stirring, until syrup reaches soft ball stage (approximately 234 to 240 degrees). Test about ½ teaspoon syrup in ice water. Syrup should easily form a ball in ice water but flatten when held in your hand. Remove from heat; stir in orange extract. Add pecans and stir until well coated. Spread pecan mixture on buttered aluminum foil. Allow to dry uncovered at room temperature 24 hours. Break apart and store in an airtight container.

Yield: about 4¼ cups pecans

HOT BACON-CHEESE DIP

3 rolls (6 ounces each) pasteurized
    process cheese food with
    garlic, quartered
2 cups sour cream
1 can (11½ ounces) bean and
    bacon soup
2 tablespoons dried chopped onion
2 teaspoons hot pepper sauce
2 teaspoons liquid smoke
2 teaspoons garlic powder
1 jar (2 ounces) real bacon pieces
Chips to serve

In a blender or food processor,
process first 7 ingredients until
smooth. Transfer cheese mixture to a
medium bowl; stir in bacon. Cover and
refrigerate 8 hours or overnight to allow
flavors to blend. Spoon dip into a large
saucepan. Stirring occasionally, cook
over medium heat until heated through.
Serve warm with chips.

Yield: about 5 cups dip

IMPERIAL CHAMPAGNE COCKTAILS

2 cups tropical fruit punch drink
2 cups orange juice
1 cup peach schnapps
1 bottle (750 ml) champagne,
    chilled

In a 2½-quart container, combine
first 3 ingredients. Cover and refrigerate
until well chilled. To serve, stir in
champagne. Serve chilled.

Yield: about ten 6-ounce servings

Imperial Champagne Cocktails are extra special when served in Elegant Etched Stemware. Hot pepper sauce and smoke flavoring add zest to our Hot Bacon-Cheese Dip.

ELEGANT ETCHED STEMWARE

For each glass (page 44), you will need a champagne flute, a 3″ square of white or clear self-adhesive plastic (Con-tact® paper), tracing paper, graphite transfer paper, masking tape, craft knife, paper towel, foam brushes, glass etching cream (available at craft stores), rubber gloves, metallic gold acrylic paint, small natural sponge piece, clear acrylic spray, and clear varnish.

1. Trace crown pattern, this page, onto tracing paper. Use transfer paper to transfer pattern onto plastic side of self-adhesive plastic.
2. Remove backing from plastic. With crown centered, place plastic on glass, smoothing bubbles or wrinkles. Cover edges of plastic with masking tape.
3. Use craft knife to cut design from plastic. Gently clean cutout areas with paper towel.
4. (*Note:* Wear rubber gloves to protect hands while using etching cream.) Follow manufacturer's instructions to apply etching cream to and remove etching cream from glass.
5. Remove tape and plastic from glass. Wash and dry glass thoroughly.
6. Use damp sponge to lightly stamp gold paint on bottom of base of glass. Allow to dry.
7. Allowing to dry between coats, apply 1 coat of acrylic spray and 1 coat of clear varnish to bottom of base of glass.
8. Glass must be hand washed.

CROWN

PARTY PLATES

For each plate (page 40), you will need a 9″ dia. clear glass plate; self-adhesive plastic (Con-tact® paper); metallic gold, purple, and dark purple acrylic paint; small natural sponge pieces; clear acrylic spray; clear varnish; and craft knife.

1. To mask off flat area on bottom of plate, draw around plate on self-adhesive plastic; cut out circle. Place plate bottom side up. Apply plastic to flat area on bottom of plate, smoothing bubbles or wrinkles. Use craft knife to trim plastic even with edge of flat area of plate. Remove excess plastic.
2. (*Note:* Allow to dry after each paint color.) On bottom of plate, use a damp sponge piece to lightly stamp gold paint on rim. Repeat with purple paint. Repeat with dark purple paint, covering rim completely.
3. Allowing to dry between coats, apply 2 coats of acrylic spray to bottom of plate.
4. Carefully remove plastic from plate, using craft knife to cut through paint along edge of plastic if necessary.
5. Apply 1 coat of clear varnish over painted area, slightly covering edges of paint. Allow to dry.
6. Plate must be hand washed.

STARRY TABLE TOPPER

For an approx. 43″ square table topper (pages 40 and 41), you will need 1¼ yds of 45″w purple fabric, gold thread and thread to match fabric, four 1⅛ yd lengths of 1⅜″w metallic gold wired ribbon, four 4½″ long gold tassels, metallic gold fabric paint, gold glitter fabric paint, acetate for stencils, stencil brush, small flat paintbrush, permanent felt-tip pen with fine point, craft knife, cutting mat or thick layer of newspapers, removable tape (optional), and paper towels.

1. Trim selvages from fabric.
2. Press edges of fabric ½″ to wrong side; press ½″ to wrong side again and stitch in place.
3. Using star patterns, page 119, and metallic gold paint, follow Stenciling, page 123, to stencil stars on table topper.
4. Use metallic gold paint to paint a ½″w border along edges of table topper; allow to dry. Apply gold glitter paint over stars as desired; allow to dry.
5. For each corner of table topper, tie 1 ribbon length into a bow; cut V-shaped notches in ribbon ends. Wrap hanging loop of 1 tassel around bow knot; tack in place. Sew bow to corner of table topper.

OLDE ENGLISH CHARM

When family and friends gather 'round the table, you can experience the warmth of a traditional English Christmas. Laughter and merriment fill the air as old times are fondly recalled. For a charming centerpiece, make our cottages and arrange them with miniatures to create a quaint little village. Shiny crackers trimmed with paper lace and ribbons hold trinkets or wrapped candy for each guest. To make the evening complete, we've compiled a menu of hearty dishes reminiscent of a feast in merry olde England.

Seafood Chowder
Roast Goose
Sausage-Pecan Stuffing
Spinach-Herb Pie
Creamy Mint Carrots
Red Cabbage and Apples
Rye Bread
Plum Pudding with Brandy Butter Sauce

Golden Roast Goose, garnished with fresh parsley and fruit, makes a magnificent showing on your holiday table. Apples and apricots lend a hint of sweetness to savory Sausage-Pecan Stuffing. Each little English Cottage is crafted from paper and trimmed with purchased miniatures.

ROAST GOOSE

1 goose (about 10 pounds)
2 tablespoons olive oil
2 cups water
2 cups apple cider, divided
¼ cup soy sauce
2 tablespoons cornstarch
2 tablespoons water

    Fresh orange slices, parsley, and
      cranberries to garnish

Remove giblets, neck, and fat from inside goose; discard fat. Preheat oven to 450 degrees. Rinse goose and pat dry. Lift wing tips up and over back so they are tucked under bird. Rub goose with oil and place breast side up in a large roasting pan. Insert meat thermometer into thickest part of thigh, making sure thermometer does not touch bone. Bake uncovered 40 to 45 minutes or until skin is crisp.

While goose is cooking, combine giblets, neck, and 2 cups water in a medium saucepan; bring to a boil, reduce heat, and simmer 30 minutes. Remove from heat and discard giblets and neck. Stir in 1 cup cider and soy sauce; set aside. Remove goose from oven; reduce oven temperature to 350 degrees. Pour cider mixture over goose. Cover with aluminum foil. Basting every 20 minutes with cider mixture, bake about 1 hour 30 minutes or until thermometer registers 180 to 185 degrees and juices run clear when thickest part of thigh is pierced with a fork. Reserve ½ cup meat drippings for sauce. Transfer goose to a serving platter and let stand 20 minutes before

48

carving. Garnish goose with orange slices, parsley, and cranberries.

For sauce, combine cornstarch and water in a small bowl; stir until smooth. In a medium saucepan, combine reserved meat drippings and remaining 1 cup cider; bring to a boil. Stirring constantly, add cornstarch mixture to sauce and cook 5 to 7 minutes or until thickened and heated through. Serve warm sauce with goose.

Yield: about 8 servings

SAUSAGE-PECAN STUFFING

1 pound mild pork sausage
1 onion, chopped
1 cup coarsely chopped celery
4 cups coarsely crumbled corn
   bread
3 cups plain croutons
3 apples, peeled, cored, and diced
1 cup chopped pecans
½ cup chopped dried apricots
2 tablespoons ground sage
2 teaspoons poultry seasoning
1 teaspoon salt
½ teaspoon ground black pepper
4 eggs, beaten
1 can (14½ ounces) chicken broth

In a medium skillet, cook sausage until brown. Reserving sausage drippings, transfer sausage to paper towels to drain; crumble. Add onion and celery to drippings in skillet; cook until tender. Remove from heat. Preheat oven to 375 degrees. In a large bowl, combine next 9 ingredients. Stir in onion mixture, sausage, eggs, and chicken broth. Spoon into a greased 9 x 13-inch pan, cover, and bake 50 minutes. Uncover and bake 10 minutes longer or until top is brown.

Yield: about 10 servings

Old-fashioned Seafood Chowder is loaded with chunks of fish, scallops, onions, and potatoes. Molasses adds richness to dark, hearty Rye Bread.

SEAFOOD CHOWDER

2 pounds orange roughy, halibut,
   or haddock fillets, cut into
   bite-size pieces
1 pound bay scallops
3 cups water
¼ pound salt pork, diced
6 onions, chopped
2 tablespoons all-purpose flour
2 cups peeled, diced red potatoes
2½ cups milk
½ cup dry white wine
½ cup finely chopped fresh parsley
2 tablespoons butter or margarine
1 teaspoon salt
1 teaspoon ground black pepper

In a large saucepan, combine fish, scallops, and water; bring to a boil over medium heat. Reduce heat and simmer 30 minutes. Reserving liquid, strain seafood.

In a stockpot, cook salt pork over medium high heat until golden brown. Reserving drippings, transfer salt pork to a bowl. Add onions to stockpot; cook until tender. Add onions to salt pork in bowl. Stir flour into drippings in stockpot and cook 1 minute. Stirring constantly, gradually add reserved seafood liquid. Add potatoes, onion mixture, and seafood. Cover and simmer over medium-low heat 40 to 45 minutes. Stir in remaining ingredients. Cook until heated through (do not boil).

Yield: about 15 servings

Dressed up with a holly sprig made from pastry scraps, this cheesy Spinach-Herb Pie is seasoned with tarragon, basil, and thyme.

SPINACH-HERB PIE

CRUST
- 1½ cups all-purpose flour
- ½ teaspoon salt
- ½ cup vegetable shortening
- ¼ cup cold water

FILLING
- 1 cup half and half
- 1 cup milk
- 4 eggs
- 1 teaspoon ground nutmeg
- 1 teaspoon salt
- ½ teaspoon ground black pepper
- ½ cup butter or margarine
- 1 onion, chopped
- 1 teaspoon dried tarragon leaves, crushed
- 1 teaspoon dried basil leaves, crushed
- 1 teaspoon dried thyme leaves, crushed
- 1 tablespoon all-purpose flour
- 2 packages (10 ounces each) frozen chopped spinach, thawed and well drained
- 1 cup (4 ounces) shredded mozzarella cheese
- 1 egg, beaten
  Green, brown, and red liquid food coloring

Trace holly pattern, page 39, onto tracing paper; cut out. For crust, combine flour and salt in a medium bowl. Using a pastry blender or 2 knives, cut in shortening until mixture resembles coarse meal. Sprinkle with water; mix until a soft dough forms. On a lightly floured surface, use a floured rolling pin to roll out dough to ⅛-inch thickness. Use a sharp knife to cut out a 9 x 13-inch rectangle and 3 holly leaves. Use knife to make veins in leaves. Shape small pieces of dough scraps into 9 berries. Reserve remaining dough scraps. Cover all dough and set aside.

Preheat oven to 350 degrees. For filling, whisk first 6 ingredients in a medium bowl. In a large skillet, melt butter over medium heat. Add onion, tarragon, basil, and thyme; cook until onion is tender. Stir in flour; cook 1 minute. Stirring constantly, gradually add half and half mixture. Cook 3 to 5 minutes or until slightly thickened. Stir in spinach. Pour filling into a greased 7 x 11-inch baking dish. Sprinkle cheese over spinach mixture. Place crust over filling and use a sharp knife to trim edge of dough. Brush crust with beaten egg. Arrange holly leaves on crust. Shape stems from reserved dough scraps and arrange on crust. Arrange berries on crust. Brush pastry decorations with beaten egg. Use a paintbrush and food coloring to paint leaves green, stems brown, and berries red. Bake 50 to 55 minutes or until crust is golden brown.

Yield: about 10 servings

CREAMY MINT CARROTS

- 5 cups thinly sliced carrots (about 1½ pounds)
- 3 cups plus 2 teaspoons water, divided
- 1 teaspoon cornstarch
- 1 cup whipping cream
- ¼ cup firmly packed brown sugar
- ¼ cup chopped fresh mint leaves
- 2 tablespoons butter or margarine
- 1 teaspoon salt
- ½ teaspoon ground black pepper

Cover carrots with 3 cups water in a large saucepan; bring to a boil. Cook carrots 3 to 5 minutes or until just tender; drain carrots and return to pan. In a small bowl, combine cornstarch and 2 teaspoons water; stir until smooth. In a small saucepan, bring cream to a boil. Whisking constantly, add cornstarch mixture to cream, bring to a boil, and cook until thickened. Stir in remaining ingredients. Stir cream mixture into carrots.

Yield: about 10 servings

RYE BREAD

- 2½ cups warm water
- ¼ cup butter or margarine, melted
- 3 packages dry yeast
- ½ cup molasses
- 2 tablespoons caraway seed
- 1 tablespoon white vinegar
- 1 teaspoon salt
- 4 cups rye flour
- 4 cups bread flour
  Vegetable cooking spray

In a large bowl, combine water and butter. Add yeast; stir until dissolved. Stir in molasses, caraway seed, vinegar, and salt. Add flours and stir until a soft dough forms. Turn onto a lightly floured surface and knead 5 minutes or until dough becomes smooth and

Served with a lightly sweetened sauce, Creamy Mint Carrots offer a delightful flavor combination. The colorful Red Cabbage and Apples is simmered in a tangy broth.

elastic. Place in a large bowl sprayed with cooking spray, turning once to coat top of dough. Cover and let rise in a warm place (80 to 85 degrees) 1 hour or until doubled in size. Turn dough onto a lightly floured surface and punch down. Divide dough into three equal pieces; shape each piece into a loaf. Place in separate 5 x 9-inch loaf pans sprayed with cooking spray; spray tops of dough. Cover and let rise in a warm place 1 hour or until doubled in size.

Preheat oven to 375 degrees. Bake 25 to 30 minutes or until bread sounds hollow when tapped. Serve warm.

Yield: 3 loaves bread

RED CABBAGE AND APPLES

- ¼ cup butter or margarine
- 2 onions, chopped
- 2 teaspoons salt
- ¾ teaspoon ground black pepper
- ½ teaspoon ground nutmeg
- 2 pounds red cabbage, chopped
- 4 apples, peeled, cored, and sliced
- 1 can (14½ ounces) chicken broth
- 3 tablespoons lemon juice
- 2 tablespoons apple cider vinegar

In a Dutch oven, melt butter over medium heat. Stir in onions, salt, pepper, and nutmeg; cook until onions are tender. Add remaining ingredients and bring to a boil. Reduce heat to medium-low, cover, and simmer 25 to 30 minutes or until cabbage and apples are tender.

Yield: about 12 servings

While the Christmas puddings of olden days often took weeks to prepare, our delectable Plum Pudding is a pleasingly modern variation. It's served with sweet Brandy Butter Sauce as a grand finale to your meal. A collar cut from wrapping paper adds a decorative touch.

PLUM PUDDING WITH BRANDY BUTTER SAUCE

PLUM PUDDING
- 1 pound pitted prunes, chopped
- 1 cup brandy
- 2½ cups all-purpose flour
- 2 teaspoons baking powder
- 1 teaspoon salt
- ½ teaspoon baking soda
- ½ teaspoon ground cinnamon
- ½ teaspoon ground cloves
- ¼ teaspoon ground nutmeg
- ¼ teaspoon ground mace
- ½ cup butter or margarine, softened
- ½ cup granulated sugar
- 3 eggs
- 1 cup molasses
- ½ teaspoon dried grated lemon peel
- 1 cup buttermilk
- 1 cup chopped walnuts

SAUCE
- 2 cups sifted confectioners sugar
- 1 cup butter or margarine
- 1 cup whipping cream
- 1 teaspoon vanilla extract
- 2 tablespoons brandy
- Ground nutmeg to garnish

For plum pudding, combine prunes and brandy in a medium bowl. Cover and let stand 8 hours or overnight.

Preheat oven to 325 degrees. In a medium bowl, sift flour, baking powder, salt, baking soda, cinnamon, cloves, nutmeg, and mace. In a large bowl, cream butter and sugar until fluffy. Add eggs, molasses, and lemon peel; beat until smooth. Beat dry ingredients and buttermilk alternately into creamed mixture. Stir in walnuts and prunes (including brandy). Pour batter into a greased and floured 9-inch springform pan. Bake 1 hour 30 minutes, cover with aluminum foil, and bake about 15 minutes longer or until a toothpick inserted in center comes out clean. Cool in pan 10 minutes; remove sides of pan.

For sauce, combine sugar, butter, cream, and vanilla in a medium saucepan. Stirring constantly, cook over medium heat until sugar dissolves and mixture comes to a boil. Stirring constantly, cook 3 minutes or until thickened. Remove from heat; stir in brandy. Garnish with nutmeg. Cut pudding into wedges and serve with warm sauce.

Yield: about 18 servings

PARTY CRACKERS

For each cracker (page 47), you will need one 7" x 13" piece each of red Mylar® gift paper and green tissue paper, a 6" length cut from a cardboard paper towel tube, a paper napkin with decorative edge, 5½" each of ⅝"w green satin ribbon and ¼"w decorative gold ribbon, two 15" lengths of 1/16" dia. gold cord, craft glue, and double-sided tape.

1. With tissue paper on top, layer gift paper and tissue paper together. Center tube along 1 long edge of papers. Roll papers around tube and tape overlapped edges together.
2. Cut two 1¾" x 5½" strips from decorative edge of napkin. Overlap long cut edges ¼" and glue together. Glue napkin border around center of cracker. Glue satin ribbon along center of napkin border; glue gold ribbon along center of satin ribbon.
3. Gather paper at 1 end of tube; tie 1 length of cord into a bow around paper to secure. Place desired favor in cracker. Gather paper at remaining end and tie with remaining cord length.

ENGLISH COTTAGES

For each cottage (page 46 or 47), you will need white poster board, clear acetate (available at craft stores), spackling compound, plastic or putty knife, craft picks (large flat toothpicks), jumbo and regular craft sticks, brown corrugated paper (available at paper supply companies), acrylic paint (see Steps 5, 8, and 14 for colors), paintbrushes, small sponge piece, light yellow spray paint, Design Master® glossy wood tone spray (available at craft stores or florist shops), loose artificial snow, miniature icicles, ⅞" dia. miniature wreath, black permanent felt-tip pen with fine point, craft knife, cutting mat or thick layer of newspapers, craft glue, hot glue gun, and glue sticks.

1. Use pen to trace desired pattern, page 116 or 117, onto acetate. Place acetate on cutting mat and use craft knife to cut along solid lines, cutting out stones or bricks as desired.
2. Draw around outer edges of acetate twice on poster board; cut out.
3. (*Note:* Follow Steps 3 - 5 for each cottage piece.) On glossy side of cottage piece, place a ruler against fold line (indicated by dotted line on pattern) and fold cottage piece.
4. Unfold cottage piece and place dull side up on a flat surface. Matching edges, place acetate pattern on cottage piece. Holding acetate firmly in place, use plastic or putty knife to spread a 1/16" thick layer of spackling compound over stone or brick cutout areas of acetate. Lifting straight up, carefully remove acetate; allow spackling compound to dry.
5. (*Note:* Allow to dry after each paint color.) For red and grey cottage, paint lower half of cottage piece red and upper half of cottage piece grey. For dark brown cottage, spray cottage piece with wood tone spray; use damp sponge piece to stamp grey paint on cottage piece. For light brown cottage, lightly spray cottage piece with wood tone spray; use damp sponge piece to stamp grey paint on cottage piece.
6. (*Note:* Use hot glue for all gluing unless otherwise indicated.) Refold cottage pieces and glue together to form cottage.
7. Lightly spray all craft picks and craft sticks with wood tone spray.
8. For door, cut a 1⅝" piece from a jumbo craft stick. If desired, paint door red or blue. Glue to cottage.
9. For front trim on each cottage, glue a 4¼" piece cut from a regular craft stick above door. For side trim on red and grey cottage, glue two 3⅞" pieces cut from regular craft sticks above bricks.
10. For windows, spray paint a section of poster board light yellow; cut desired windows from poster board. Use pen and a ruler to draw lines for window panes. Glue windows to cottage.
11. For shutters, use pen to draw lines across regular craft sticks. Cut sticks to fit sides of windows and glue to cottage. For window frames, cut craft picks and craft sticks to fit around windows and glue to cottage.
12. For roof, glue two 3¼" x 5" pieces of corrugated paper to cottage.
13. Cut 2 lengths of icicles same length as bottom edge of roof; glue along bottom edges of roof. Glue wreath to door.
14. For base, cut an irregular piece of poster board. Glue cottage to base. For walkway, paint a small section of base in front of door grey.
15. For snow, use paintbrush to apply a thin layer of craft glue to rooftop. Sprinkle snow on rooftop. Allow to dry; shake off excess snow. Sprinkle more snow on base around house; clear snow from walkway.

SHOPPERS' BRUNCH-N-GO

To kick off a day of Christmas shopping, why not start with a glitzy brunch! Impressive "credit card" invitations will charge your guests with excitement. Gaily wrapped packages and foil gift bags overflowing with "fun money" make a colorful centerpiece that will inspire holiday shopaholics. To help carry home their purchases, you'll provide festively trimmed tote bags for favors. Our menu features a variety of delightful dishes to fortify hungry shoppers.

Caviar Mousse

Feta Cheese-Vegetable Salad

Chicken-Cucumber Salad

Chocolate Bread Pudding with Caramel Sauce

Hot Berry-Brandy Punch

Served atop cucumber slices, Caviar Mousse makes an elegant appetizer. The flavorful Feta Cheese-Vegetable Salad features crisp fresh vegetables with a tangy buttermilk-and-basil dressing.

CAVIAR MOUSSE

1 teaspoon unflavored gelatin
2 tablespoons cold water
2 tablespoons boiling water
2 tablespoons mayonnaise
½ tablespoon finely chopped fresh
    dill weed *or* ½ teaspoon
    dried dill weed
1 teaspoon lemon juice
1 teaspoon finely chopped onion
¼ teaspoon hot pepper sauce
¼ teaspoon paprika
1 jar (2 ounces) red lumpfish
    caviar, well drained
¼ cup heavy cream
2 large cucumbers
    Fresh dill weed to garnish

Place a medium bowl and beaters from an electric mixer in freezer. In another medium bowl, combine gelatin and cold water. Add boiling water and stir until gelatin dissolves. Cool to room temperature. Whisk in mayonnaise, dill weed, lemon juice, onion, pepper sauce, and paprika. Cover and refrigerate 5 minutes or until slightly thickened. Fold caviar into gelatin mixture.

In chilled bowl, whip cream until stiff peaks form. Fold whipped cream into caviar mixture. Cover and chill 2 hours or until set. Reserving ¼ of 1 cucumber, slice remaining cucumbers into ¼-inch-thick slices. Spoon rounded teaspoonfuls of caviar mixture onto cucumber slices. Cut reserved ¼ cucumber into ⅛-inch-thick slices and then into quarters. Garnish each appetizer with a cucumber quarter and 1 piece of dill weed.

Yield: about 1½ dozen appetizers

FETA CHEESE-VEGETABLE SALAD

DRESSING
1 cup chopped fresh basil leaves *or*
    2 tablespoons dried basil
    leaves, crushed
¾ cup balsamic vinegar
⅔ cup buttermilk
⅓ cup olive oil
1 tablespoon Dijon-style mustard
2 teaspoons salt
1 teaspoon ground black pepper
½ teaspoon garlic powder
SALAD
3 cups fresh broccoli flowerets
3 cups shredded green cabbage
2 cups thinly sliced zucchini
1½ cups sliced red onions
1½ cups thinly sliced carrots
10 ounces crumbled feta cheese
    (about 1½ cups)

For dressing, combine all ingredients in a 1-pint jar with a tight fitting lid. Shake until well blended. Refrigerate 8 hours or overnight to allow flavors to blend.

In a large bowl, combine vegetables. Pour dressing over vegetables; stir until well coated. Stir in cheese.

Yield: about 12 cups salad

CHICKEN-CUCUMBER SALAD

1½ pounds boneless, skinless
     chicken breasts
  1 package (8 ounces) cream cheese,
     softened
  ½ cup sour cream
  2 tablespoons dry white wine
1½ teaspoons garlic powder
  1 teaspoon salt
  ½ teaspoon ground black pepper
  ½ teaspoon dried dill weed
  ½ teaspoon hot pepper sauce
  1 cup peeled, diced cucumber
  ½ cup chopped green onions
  4 acorn squash, halved lengthwise
     and seeded
     Fresh carrot and green
      pepper slices to garnish

In a medium saucepan, cover
chicken with water. Bring to a boil,
reduce heat to medium-low, and simmer
30 to 35 minutes or until chicken is
done; drain. Cool 10 minutes and cut
into bite-size pieces.

In a medium bowl, beat cream cheese
and sour cream until fluffy. Beat in next
6 ingredients. Stir in chicken,
cucumber, and onions. Cut a thin slice
off bottom of each squash half so squash
will sit level. Spoon chicken salad into
each squash half. Refer to photo and
garnish with carrot and green pepper
slices. Cover and refrigerate until ready
to serve.

Yield: 8 servings

HOT BERRY-BRANDY PUNCH

  2 packages (12 ounces each) frozen
     raspberries, thawed
  1 gallon cranberry juice cocktail
  2 cups granulated sugar
  2 cups blackberry-flavored brandy
  ½ cup raspberry-flavored liqueur

Cool, creamy Chicken-Cucumber Salad is attractively presented in acorn squash halves. Hot Berry-Brandy Punch is deliciously fruity.

In blender or food processor, purée
raspberries. Strain; discard seeds and
pulp. In a Dutch oven, combine
raspberry purée and remaining
ingredients. Bring to a boil, stirring until
sugar dissolves. Serve warm.

Yield: about twenty-six 6-ounce
servings

This Chocolate Bread Pudding is an old-fashioned favorite with a chocolate twist! A drizzling of warm Caramel Sauce makes the moist dessert irresistible.

CHOCOLATE BREAD PUDDING WITH CARAMEL SAUCE

BREAD PUDDING
- 1 can (10 biscuits) refrigerated buttermilk biscuits, baked according to package directions
- 2 cups milk
- 2 eggs
- 2 tablespoons butter or margarine, melted
- 2 teaspoons vanilla extract
- ¾ cup granulated sugar
- ¼ cup cocoa
- ½ cup semisweet chocolate chips

CARAMEL SAUCE
- ½ cup butter or margarine
- ½ cup firmly packed brown sugar
- ½ cup granulated sugar
- ½ cup evaporated milk
- 1 tablespoon vanilla extract

For bread pudding, preheat oven to 350 degrees. Tear baked biscuits into bite-size pieces. In a large bowl, combine biscuits and milk; set aside.

In a medium bowl, beat eggs, butter, and vanilla until well blended. Add sugar and cocoa; beat until well blended. Stir in chocolate chips. Add chocolate mixture to biscuit mixture; stir until well blended. Pour into a greased 8-inch square glass baking dish. Bake 55 to 60 minutes or until set in center and edges pull away from sides of pan.

For sauce, combine butter, sugars, and milk in a medium saucepan. Stirring constantly, cook over low heat until butter melts and sugars dissolve. Increase heat to medium and bring to a boil. Stirring constantly, boil about 9 minutes or until thickened. Remove from heat; stir in vanilla. Cut warm bread pudding into squares and serve with warm sauce.

Yield: about 9 servings

SHOPPING TOTES

For each tote (this page), you will need a purchased tote, an 8″ x 10″ piece of gold metallic knit fabric, a 5″ x 8″ piece of silver metallic knit fabric, paper-backed fusible web, decorative ribbons, acrylic jewels, jewel glue, metallic gold fabric paint, small paintbrush, black permanent felt-tip pen with fine point, and tracing paper.

1. Follow manufacturer's instructions to fuse web to wrong sides of fabrics.
2. Trace credit card pattern, page 119, onto tracing paper; cut out.
3. Use pattern to cut 2 credit cards from gold fabric and 1 from silver fabric.
4. Arrange credit cards as desired on front of tote; fuse in place.
5. On top credit card, use pen to write "Preferred" at top and guest's name at bottom. Arrange jewels and ribbon lengths on cards; glue in place. Allow to dry.
6. Use a pencil to write "Cardholders have more fun!" on tote. Use fabric paint to paint over words. Allow to dry.
7. Glue ribbon lengths along centers of tote handles; glue ribbon lengths over seams and along top edge of tote. Allow to dry.

To help your fellow shoppers carry their purchases home in style, trim oversized Shopping Totes with shiny metallic ribbon and replicas of the credit card-inspired invitations.

SHOPPERS' INVITATIONS AND ENVELOPES

For each invitation and envelope (page 54), you will need a 7″ x 9″ piece of cream-colored cover stock paper, a matching 4½″ x 6½″ envelope, an 8″ x 15″ piece of gold metallic knit fabric, paper-backed fusible web, decorative ribbons, acrylic jewels, jewel glue, black permanent felt-tip pen with fine point, and tracing paper.

1. Follow manufacturer's instructions to fuse web to wrong side of fabric.
2. Trace credit card pattern, page 119, onto tracing paper; cut out.
3. Use pattern to cut 1 credit card from fabric. Set aside remaining fabric.
4. For invitation, match short edges and fold paper in half. Match 1 long edge of credit card to fold of paper and fuse in place. Cut out invitation along side and bottom edges of credit card.
5. Use pen to write "Preferred Shopper" near top on front of invitation. Arrange jewels and ribbon lengths on invitation; glue in place. Allow to dry.
6. For envelope, use opened envelope as a pattern to cut a piece from remaining fabric. Place fabric in envelope, trimming side edges to fit. Trim fabric to expose gummed edge of envelope. Fuse fabric to inside of envelope.

SUGAR AND SPICE TEA

*Capturing the charm
of childhood tea parties,
this holiday gathering is
a special occasion for
mothers, daughters, and
grandmothers. The three
generations can enjoy each
others' company and share
memories while sampling
treats from our lavish
dessert buffet. Setting an
old-fashioned mood, a
darling bear couple clad
in Victorian style enjoys
a tea party at a tiny table.
A dainty tabletop tree
adorned with feminine
frills completes the
enchanting centerpiece.*

Chocolate-Orange Tea Cakes

Amaretto Cream Napoleons

Brandy Pound Cake with Spun Sugar

Chocolate Custard

Peanut Butter-Cinnamon Brownies

Banana-Pecan Tart

Santa Cookies

Black Forest Cheesecake

Mocha-Carrot Cake

Spiced Apple Punch

SPICED APPLE PUNCH

- 2 teaspoons ground cinnamon
- 1 teaspoon dried grated lemon peel
- 1/4 teaspoon ground cloves
- 1/4 teaspoon ground allspice
- 1/4 teaspoon ground nutmeg
- 1 gallon apple cider
- 1 liter ginger ale, chilled
- 2 Red Delicious apples, cut crosswise into 1/4-inch slices, and cinnamon sticks to garnish

Place spices in a 6-inch square of cheesecloth or a coffee filter and tie with string. Pour cider into a stockpot. Add bundle of spices. Stirring occasionally, cook over medium-low heat 1 1/2 hours. Remove from heat; cool to room temperature. Remove spice bundle and discard. Place punch in a covered container and freeze.

Remove punch from freezer 4 hours before serving to partially thaw. To serve, break into chunks, add ginger ale, and stir until slushy. Ladle into glasses and garnish with apple slices and cinnamon sticks.

Yield: about twenty-two 6-ounce servings

CHOCOLATE-ORANGE TEA CAKES

CAKES
- 1 box (18.25 ounces) devil's food cake mix without pudding
- 1 box (3.9 ounces) chocolate instant pudding and pie filling mix
- 3 eggs
- 1 1/4 cups water
- 1/2 cup vegetable oil
- 2 teaspoons orange extract

ICING
- 1 1/2 cups whipping cream
- 2 1/4 cups semisweet chocolate chips
- 1 teaspoon orange extract

  Purchased white decorating icing to decorate

For cakes, preheat oven to 350 degrees. In a large bowl, combine cake mix, pudding mix, eggs, water, oil, and orange extract. Using low speed of an electric mixer, beat until moistened. Increase speed of mixer to medium and beat 2 minutes longer. Pour batter into a greased and lightly floured 10 x 15-inch jellyroll pan. Bake 20 to 25 minutes or until a toothpick inserted in center of cake comes out clean. Cool in pan 5 minutes. Remove from pan and cool completely on a wire rack. Place on waxed paper. Use a 2-inch heart-shaped cookie cutter to cut out cakes.

For icing, place cream in a medium saucepan; bring to a boil over medium heat. Remove from heat; add chocolate chips and orange extract. Let stand 1 minute. Whisk until smooth. Cool 5 minutes. Placing cakes on a fork, dip cakes one at a time into icing and place on a wire rack with waxed paper underneath. Spoon decorating icing into a pastry bag fitted with a small round tip. Pipe icing on tops of cakes. Store in an airtight container in refrigerator.

Yield: about 2 dozen tea cakes

AMARETTO CREAM NAPOLEONS

PASTRIES
- 2 sheets (one 17 1/4-ounce package) frozen puff pastry, thawed according to package directions
- 1 can (20 ounces) evaporated milk
- 1 1/2 cups granulated sugar
- 5 tablespoons all-purpose flour
- 4 egg yolks
- 2 tablespoons butter or margarine
- 1/2 cup amaretto
- 1 teaspoon vanilla extract
- 1 teaspoon almond extract

ICING
- 2 1/4 cups sifted confectioners sugar
- 3 tablespoons milk
- 1/4 cup semisweet chocolate chips

For pastries, preheat oven to 400 degrees. On a lightly floured surface, cut puff pastry into 2 x 3-inch rectangles. Place rectangles on an ungreased baking sheet. Bake 18 to 20 minutes or until golden brown. Cool completely on a wire rack.

In a medium saucepan, combine milk, sugar, flour, egg yolks, and butter. Stirring constantly, bring to a boil over medium heat; boil 2 to 3 minutes or until thickened. Remove from heat. Stir in amaretto and extracts. Cover and refrigerate until well chilled.

Carefully lift off tops of pastries. Generously spoon amaretto mixture on bottoms of pastries. Replace tops.

For icing, combine sugar and milk; stir until smooth. Generously spread icing on top of each pastry. Allow icing to harden.

In a small saucepan, melt chocolate chips over low heat, stirring constantly. Spoon chocolate into a pastry bag fitted with a small round tip. Pipe chocolate on top of each pastry. Allow chocolate to harden. Store in an airtight container in refrigerator.

Yield: about 2 dozen napoleons

BRANDY POUND CAKE WITH SPUN SUGAR

CAKE
- 1 cup butter or margarine, softened
- 1 1/2 cups granulated sugar

Swirls of spun sugar create a colorful crown for spicy Brandy Pound Cake. Shown on page 60: Heart-shaped Chocolate-Orange Tea Cakes are moist and rich, and flaky Amaretto Cream Napoleons have a sweet, creamy filling. Apple slices and cinnamon sticks garnish glasses of frosty Spiced Apple Punch.

5 eggs
2 tablespoons brandy
1 tablespoon vanilla extract
1½ cups all-purpose flour
2 teaspoons ground ginger
1 teaspoon baking powder
½ teaspoon baking soda
½ teaspoon ground nutmeg
¼ teaspoon ground mace
¼ teaspoon salt

CING
½ cup water
2 tablespoons light corn syrup
6½ cups sifted confectioners sugar
1 teaspoon vanilla extract
20 red hard candies for spun sugar

For cake, preheat oven to
25 degrees. In a large bowl, cream butter and sugar until fluffy. Add eggs, one at a time, beating well after each addition. Beat in brandy and vanilla. In a medium bowl, sift next 7 ingredients. Add dry ingredients to creamed mixture; beat until well blended. Pour batter into a greased and floured 10-inch tube pan. Bake 1 hour to 1 hour 5 minutes, testing for doneness with a toothpick. Cool in pan 15 minutes; remove from pan. Cool completely on a wire rack with waxed paper underneath.

For icing, combine water and corn syrup in a medium saucepan. Stir in sugar until well blended. Attach candy thermometer to pan, making sure thermometer does not touch bottom of pan. Stirring constantly, cook over medium-low heat until icing reaches 100 degrees. Remove from heat; stir in vanilla. Cool icing 5 minutes. Ice top and sides of cake. Allow icing to harden.

In a small saucepan, melt candies over medium heat, stirring occasionally with a fork. When syrup begins to form a thread, remove from heat. Dip fork into syrup and allow threads of syrup to fall onto a piece of ungreased aluminum foil, forming a 10-inch circle. Reheating syrup as necessary, repeat procedure with remaining syrup to form several layers of spun sugar. Allow spun sugar to harden; place on cake. Store in an airtight container.

Yield: about 16 servings

Incredibly rich Chocolate Custard is topped with chocolate curls and sweetened whipped cream. Moist, chewy Peanut Butter-Cinnamon Brownies feature an unusual flavor combination.

CHOCOLATE CUSTARD

CUSTARD
- 3 eggs, beaten
- 1 cup (6 ounces) semisweet chocolate chips
- 1½ cups milk
- ½ cup granulated sugar
- ¼ teaspoon ground cinnamon

CHOCOLATE CURLS
- 1 cup (6 ounces) semisweet chocolate chips

DECORATIVE TOPPING
- 2 tablespoons water
- 1½ teaspoons unflavored gelatin
- 2 tablespoons granulated sugar
- ½ cup whipping cream

For custard, preheat oven to 325 degrees. Place eggs in a small bowl. In a medium saucepan, melt chocolate chips over low heat. Stir in milk, sugar, and cinnamon. Increase heat to medium. Stirring constantly, bring to a simmer and cook until sugar dissolves. Add about ½ cup chocolate mixture to eggs; stir until well blended. Gradually add egg mixture to chocolate mixture in saucepan, stirring until well blended. Remove from heat. Place a greased 9-inch pie plate in a shallow roasting pan. Pour chocolate mixture into pie plate. Fill roasting pan with very hot water to come halfway up side of pie plate. Bake 55 to 60 minutes or until a knife inserted near center of custard comes out clean. Cool completely on a wire rack. Cover and refrigerate until well chilled.

For chocolate curls, melt chocolate chips in a small saucepan over low heat, stirring constantly. Pour onto an ungreased baking sheet, spreading chocolate to form a 3 x 6-inch rectangle. Refrigerate until set but not firm. To make curls, pull a chocolate curler or vegetable peeler across surface of chocolate (curls will break if chocolate is too firm). Remelt and cool chocolate as necessary to form desired number of curls. Refrigerate curls until ready to decorate.

For decorative topping, place a medium bowl and beaters from an electric mixer in freezer until well chilled. In a small bowl, combine water and gelatin; let stand 1 minute. In a small saucepan, combine gelatin mixture and sugar; cook over low heat, stirring until gelatin and sugar dissolve. Remove from heat. In chilled bowl, beat cream until soft peaks form. Add sugar mixture and beat until stiff peaks form. Spoon topping into a pastry bag fitted with a large star tip. Pipe a decorative border on top of custard. Garnish with chocolate curls. Store in an airtight container in refrigerator.

Yield: about 10 servings

PEANUT BUTTER-CINNAMON BROWNIES

- ¼ cup butter or margarine, melted
- ½ cup granulated sugar
- ½ cup firmly packed brown sugar
- 2 eggs
- 1 teaspoon vanilla extract
- ½ cup all-purpose flour
- 1 teaspoon ground cinnamon

½ teaspoon baking powder
½ teaspoon salt
½ cup extra-crunchy peanut butter

Preheat oven to 350 degrees. In a medium bowl, combine butter and sugars. Add eggs and vanilla; beat until smooth. In a small bowl, combine flour, cinnamon, baking powder, and salt. Add dry ingredients to butter mixture; stir just until dry ingredients are moistened. Stir in peanut butter. Spread batter into a greased 7 x 11-inch metal baking pan. Bake 20 to 25 minutes or until set in center. Cool completely in pan. Cut into squares to serve.

Yield: about 2 dozen brownies

BANANA-PECAN TART

CRUST

1¾ cups graham cracker crumbs
⅓ cup all-purpose flour
⅓ cup granulated sugar
6 tablespoons butter or margarine, melted

FILLING

3 ripe bananas, sliced
½ cup granulated sugar
¼ cup light corn syrup
2 eggs
4 tablespoons butter or margarine, melted
1 tablespoon vanilla extract
1 teaspoon imitation rum extract
2 ounces semisweet baking chocolate, melted
1½ cups chopped pecans
1 package (6 ounces) semisweet chocolate chips, divided

For crust, combine all ingredients in a medium bowl until well blended. Press into bottom and up sides of a greased 8 x 11-inch tart pan with removable bottom; set aside.

Bananas, chocolate, and pecans are nestled in a graham cracker crust to create this delectable Banana-Pecan Tart.

Preheat oven to 350 degrees. For filling, arrange banana slices in single layer in crust. In a large bowl, whisk sugar, corn syrup, eggs, butter, and extracts. Whisk in melted chocolate. Stir in pecans and ½ cup chocolate chips. Pour chocolate mixture over bananas. Bake 45 to 50 minutes or until top is dry and slightly cracked. Cool 15 minutes on a wire rack. Remove sides of pan and cool completely.

To decorate, place remaining ½ cup chocolate chips in a disposable pastry bag and microwave on medium power (50%) for 30 second intervals until melted. Cut tip of pastry bag to form a small hole and drizzle chocolate over top of tart. Allow chocolate to harden. Cut into squares to serve.

Yield: about 12 servings

Beautifully decorated with icing and food coloring, each Santa Cookie is a little work of art. The buttery cookies, shaped in a cookie mold, are richly spiced with coriander.

SANTA COOKIES

COOKIES

    1 cup butter or margarine, softened
    1 cup firmly packed brown sugar
    ½ cup granulated sugar
    1 egg
    1 teaspoon vanilla extract
    3½ cups all-purpose flour
    1 teaspoon ground coriander
    ¼ teaspoon salt

ICING

    6 tablespoons sifted confectioners
        sugar
    4 teaspoons milk
        Burgundy, green, and black paste
        food coloring

Preheat oven to 350 degrees. For cookies, cream butter and sugars in a medium bowl until fluffy. Add egg and vanilla; beat until smooth. In a small bowl, combine flour, coriander, and salt. Add dry ingredients to creamed mixture; stir until a soft dough forms.

Press small pieces of dough into a greased and lightly floured cookie mold. Use a sharp knife to loosen edges of dough. Invert mold onto a greased baking sheet. Tap edge of mold lightly to release dough. Repeat for remaining dough. Bake 10 to 12 minutes or until edges of cookies are brown. Transfer to a wire rack to cool completely.

For icing, combine sugar and milk until smooth. To decorate cookies, dilute food coloring with a small amount of water. Referring to photo, use a paintbrush to paint food coloring on each cookie. Use a clean paintbrush to brush white icing on cookie for beard, mustache, eyebrows, and trim on coat, hat, and sled. Brush icing lightly over each sled. Allow icing to harden. Store in an airtight container.

Yield: about 1 dozen 5-inch cookies

BLACK FOREST CHEESECAKE

Cheesecake must be made 1 day in advance.

CHOCOLATE DECORATIONS

    ½ cup semisweet chocolate chips

CRUST

    1 package (12 ounces) vanilla wafer
        cookies, finely crushed
    ¾ cup butter or margarine, melted

FILLING

    1 package (12 ounces) semisweet
        chocolate chips, divided
    20 ounces (two and one-half
        8-ounce packages) cream
        cheese, softened
    ¾ cup granulated sugar
    3 eggs
    1 egg yolk
    2 teaspoons all-purpose flour
    1 tablespoon vanilla extract
    2 tablespoons whipping cream

TOPPING

    2 cans (16 ounces each) tart red
        pitted cherries, undrained
    ¼ cup cornstarch
    1 cup granulated sugar

DECORATIVE TOPPING

    2 tablespoons water
    1½ teaspoons unflavored gelatin
    2 tablespoons granulated sugar
    ½ cup whipping cream
        Maraschino cherries with stems

For chocolate decorations, melt chocolate chips in a small saucepan over low heat, stirring constantly. Spoon chocolate into a pastry bag fitted with a small round tip. For each decoration, pipe chocolate onto waxed paper, forming a 2½-inch-high triangle. Randomly pipe chocolate inside triangle, making sure piped lines overlap. Repeat to make 16 decorations. Allow chocolate to

A wonderful variation of a favorite dessert, Black Forest Cheesecake is a luscious chocolate cheesecake with a sweet cherry topping. Each slice is topped with whipped cream, a cherry, and a delicate chocolate lattice.

harden. Store in a cool, dry place until ready to decorate.

For crust, combine cookie crumbs and butter. Press into bottom and halfway up sides of a greased 9-inch springform pan. Cover and refrigerate.

For filling, melt 1 cup chocolate chips in a small saucepan over low heat, stirring constantly; remove from heat. Adding 1 package at a time, beat cream cheese for 25 minutes in a large bowl. Preheat oven to 500 degrees. Add sugar and melted chocolate to cream cheese; beat 5 minutes longer. Add eggs and egg yolk, one at a time, beating 2 minutes after each addition. Beat in flour, vanilla, and cream. Stir in remaining 1 cup chocolate chips. Pour filling into crust. Bake 10 minutes.

Reduce heat to 200 degrees. Bake 1 hour. Turn oven off and leave cake in oven 1 hour without opening door. Cool completely on a wire rack. Remove sides of pan.

For topping, drain canned cherries, reserving ¼ cup juice. In a small bowl, combine cornstarch and reserved cherry juice. In a medium saucepan, combine cherries and sugar. Stirring occasionally, cook over medium heat until sugar dissolves and mixture comes to a boil. Stirring constantly, add cornstarch mixture and cook until thickened. Remove from heat; cool to room temperature. Spoon cherry mixture over cheesecake. Store in an airtight container 8 hours or overnight in refrigerator.

For decorative topping, place a large bowl and beaters from an electric mixer in freezer until well chilled. In a small bowl, combine water and gelatin; let stand 1 minute. In a small saucepan, combine gelatin mixture and sugar; cook over low heat, stirring until gelatin and sugar dissolve. Remove from heat. In chilled bowl, beat cream until soft peaks form. Add sugar mixture and beat until stiff peaks form. Spoon whipped cream mixture into a pastry bag fitted with a large star tip and pipe on cake. Carefully peel waxed paper from chocolate decorations. Place chocolate decorations and cherries on cake. Store in an airtight container in refrigerator.

Yield: about 16 servings

Coffee-flavored liqueur adds richness to delicious Mocha-Carrot Cake. For charming mementos of the day, give each guest a cross-stitched Sugar and Spice Tote filled with candy canes and a tiny teddy bear.

MOCHA-CARROT CAKE

CAKE

- 2 cups granulated sugar
- ¾ cup vegetable oil
- ½ cup coffee-flavored liqueur
- 4 eggs
- 3 cups sifted all-purpose flour
- 1 tablespoon baking powder
- 1½ teaspoons ground cinnamon
- ½ teaspoon salt
- 3 cups shredded carrots
- 1 cup chopped walnuts
- ½ cup raisins

FROSTING

- 6 cups sifted confectioners sugar
- 2 packages (8 ounces each) cream cheese, softened
- 1 cup butter or margarine, softened
- 1 cup finely chopped walnuts

For cake, preheat oven to 350 degrees. In a large bowl, combine sugar, oil, liqueur, and eggs. Using high speed of an electric mixer, beat 3 minutes. In a medium bowl, sift flour, baking powder, cinnamon, and salt. Add dry ingredients to sugar mixture; beat until well blended. Stir in carrots, walnuts, and raisins. Pour batter into 2 greased and floured 9-inch cake pans. Bake 30 to 35 minutes or until a toothpick inserted in center of cake comes out clean. Cool in pans

10 minutes. Remove from pans and cool completely on a wire rack.

For frosting, combine first three ingredients in a large bowl; beat until smooth. Reserving 1½ cups frosting, spread remaining frosting between layer and on sides and top of cake.

To decorate cake, sprinkle walnuts on top of cake. Spoon reserved frosting into a pastry bag fitted with a small star tip. Pipe stripes of frosting 1 inch apart on top of cake in a lattice design. Pipe a decorative border around top and bottom edges of cake. Store in an airtight container in refrigerator.

Yield: about 16 servings

Dressed in darling handmade outfits, our Teddy Bear Couple poses with some little friends beside the dainty tabletop tree.

TEA PARTY CENTERPIECE

This sweet centerpiece (pages 60 and 61) is sure to be enjoyed by ladies of all ages. Our Teddy Bear Couple (this page) is dressed for the occasion in fancy clothes that are easy to make. Our boy bear's tuxedo features a shirt made from folded paper and a jacket tailored from velvet ribbon. His sweetheart's dress has a Battenberg doily collar for a feminine touch.

The bears' tea table is actually a bucket covered with a circle of colorful fabric, which we topped with our cross-stitched Table Topper (page 71). We covered the pads of the 9½" high purchased chairs with coordinating fabric.

A tiny Christmas tree provides a cheerful atmosphere for the tea party. The pot at the base of the 2-foot-tall tree was wrapped with batting and then covered with a 30" square of fabric which was secured with satin ribbon tied into a bow at the top of the pot. Along with paper roses and silk flowers, pearl bead garland adds a delicate touch to the tree. Chandelier prisms purchased from an antique shop were tied to the tree with satin ribbons to make pretty ornaments. Sprigs of holly provide bright patches of color. A length of organdy ribbon tied into a bow makes a perfect topper for our tea party tree.

TEDDY BEAR COUPLE

For boy bear (this page), you will need a 12" tall jointed teddy bear; two 10" lengths of 3"w wired velvet ribbon for jacket; 14" of 1"w black satin ribbon, ½ yd of ⅝"w black satin ribbon, and 6" of ¼"w black satin ribbon for cummerbund, tie, and hatband; thread to match ribbons; plain white paper; 4 black seed beads for buttons; purchased 3"w gold wire doll glasses and 2" dia. felt hat; and craft glue.

For girl bear (this page), you will need a 12" tall jointed teddy bear, a 10" x 33" piece of fabric for dress, 33" of 2"w pregathered eyelet trim, ½ yd of ⅝"w satin ribbon, thread to match fabric and ribbon, a 6" square Battenberg lace doily, 1 medium and 3 small ribbon roses, and fabric glue.

BOY BEAR

1. For shirt pleats, cut 4 strips of paper 4" long and the following widths: 1½", 2", 2½", and 3". Fold long edges of each strip ½" to 1 side (wrong side) and crease at folds. Layer strips right side up from widest to narrowest and glue strips together.
2. For shirt, cut a 4" x 6" piece of paper. Matching short edges of pleats to long edges of paper piece, center and glue pleats to paper piece. Allow to dry. Trim 1 long edge (top) and sides of shirt to fit under bear's chin and arms; trim bottom of shirt even with waistline.
3. For cummerbund, center and glue 1"w ribbon along bottom edge of shirt.

Continued on page 70

69

6. For side seams, fold each ribbon length in half, matching wrong sides and ends (Fig. 2); whipstitch ribbons together 1″ along each side edge to form armholes.

Fig. 2

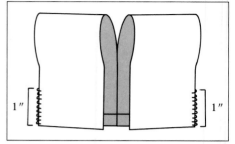

7. Place shirt on bear. Wrap cummerbund around bear; tack in place. Wrap tie around neck, covering top edge of shirt; tack in place. Glue beads to shirt; allow to dry. Place jacket and glasses on bear. For hatband, glue remaining ¼″w ribbon around hat; glue hat to head.

GIRL BEAR

1. For dress, match wrong sides and fold fabric piece in half lengthwise.
2. For trim, glue straight edge of eyelet to 1 side (wrong side) of dress so that 1″ of eyelet extends beyond folded edge (bottom) of dress; allow to dry.
3. Matching right sides and short edges, fold fabric piece in half. Glue short edges together; allow to dry. Turn right side out.
4. Baste ¼″ from top edge of dress. Place dress on bear under bear's arms; pull basting threads, gathering fabric to fit bear. Knot threads and trim ends.
5. For collar, cut from 1 corner of doily to center; cut a circle from center to fit bear's neck. Glue small roses to collar. Place collar around neck; tack in place.
6. For bow, form a double-loop bow from ribbon; tack remaining rose to center of bow. Glue bow to bear's head.

No one will guess that this miniature tea table is really a bucket covered with a circle of floral fabric! The cross-stitched Table Topper is edged with lace and trimmed with a pretty bow at each corner.

4. For tie, cut a 6″ length of ⅝″w ribbon and a 1″ length of ¼″w ribbon. Overlapping ends 1″, form a loop from 6″ ribbon length; tack ends together. Flatten loop and center on remaining ⅝″w ribbon length. Wrap 1″ ribbon length around center of loop and ribbon; tack in place.
5. For jacket, fold ends of each length of wired ribbon ½″ to wrong side and glue in place. For back seam, place ribbon lengths wrong sides together; whipstitch ribbons together 1½″ along 1 long edge (Fig. 1).

Fig. 1

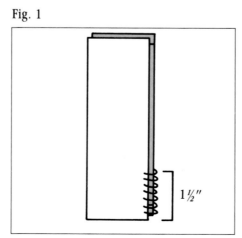

1½″

TABLE TOPPER

For table topper (page 70), you will need one 16″ square of Rose Aida (14 ct), embroidery floss (see color key), embroidery hoop (optional), 2 yds of ⅜″w lace trim, four 12″ lengths of ⅝″w satin ribbon, and fabric glue.

1. With design centered and bottom of design ¾″ from 1 edge, of fabric, work border design on fabric, using 3 strands of floss for Cross Stitch, 2 for ecru Backstitch, and 1 for remaining

Backstitch. Repeat design to 2¾″ from each edge, completing partial figures at each end. Repeat for remaining edges of fabric.

2. Press edges of table topper ⅜″ to wrong side; glue in place. Glue straight edge of lace along edges on wrong side of table topper. Allow to dry.

3. Tie each ribbon length into a bow. Glue bows to corners of table topper; allow to dry.

SUGAR AND SPICE TOTE

For each tote (page 68), you will need one Rose Aida (14 ct) Lil' Tote (5″ x 5″) and embroidery floss (see color key).

With top of design ½″ from top edge of tote, work design on tote, using 3 strands of floss for Cross Stitch, 2 for ecru and green Backstitch, 1 for remaining Backstitch, and 2 for French Knot.

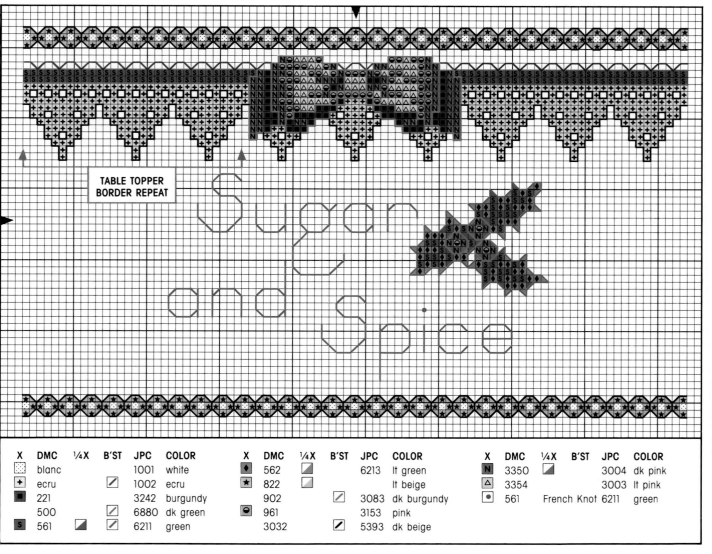

TABLE TOPPER BORDER REPEAT

X	DMC	¼X	B'ST	JPC	COLOR	X	DMC	¼X	B'ST	JPC	COLOR	X	DMC	¼X	B'ST	JPC	COLOR
	blanc			1001	white	◆	562	◪		6213	lt green	N	3350	◪		3004	dk pink
+	ecru		◪	1002	ecru	★	822	◪			lt beige	△	3354			3003	lt pink
■	221			3242	burgundy		902		◪	3083	dk burgundy	●	561		French Knot	6211	green
	500		◪	6880	dk green	◉	961			3153	pink						
S	561	◪	◪	6211	green		3032		◪	5393	dk beige						

"JUST FOR KIDS" SKATING PARTY

Kids will love this Christmasy skating party! The cute invitations boldly announce the theme with a crafty skate-shaped cutout. On arrival, each child will receive a party cap decorated with ribbon and sequins for girls or plaid fabric for boys. To make the excursion even merrier, our menu features treats that travel easily — so the party can be held right at the rink. And when it's time to go home, there's a bear-shaped popcorn snack to carry along. This celebration on wheels is sure to be tons of fun!

Orange-Pineapple Punch

"Beary" Christmas Popcorn Snacks

Crunchy Party Mix

Pecan Shortbread Cookies

A yummy cinnamon-sugar coating adds sweetness to Crunchy Party Mix. The clever Skating Party Invitations have star-studded wheels, a cottony pom-pom, and real laces. Shown on previous page: Slushy Orange-Pineapple Punch has a fruity flavor that kids will love, and "Beary" Christmas Popcorn Snacks are tucked in cellophane Favor Bags.

ORANGE-PINEAPPLE PUNCH

Punch must be made 1 day in advance.

- 2 quarts water
- 2 cans (20 ounces each) unsweetened crushed pineapple, undrained
- 3 cups granulated sugar
- 3 ripe bananas, mashed
- 1 can (12 ounces) frozen orange juice concentrate, thawed
- 1 can (6 ounces) frozen lemonade concentrate, thawed
- 1 package (0.14 ounces) unsweetened orange-flavored soft drink mix
- 1 liter ginger ale, chilled
- 1 jar (10 ounces) maraschino cherries, drained

In a 6-quart container, combine first 7 ingredients. Place punch in a covered container and freeze.

Remove punch from freezer 4 hours before serving to partially thaw. To serve, break into chunks. Add ginger ale and cherries; stir until slushy.

Yield: about twenty-seven 6-ounce servings

"BEARY" CHRISTMAS POPCORN SNACKS

- 16 cups popped popcorn
- 4 cups miniature marshmallows
- ¼ cup butter or margarine
- 2 tablespoons milk
- ½ cup smooth peanut butter
- 1 tablespoon vanilla extract
- 1 teaspoon salt
  Miniature chocolate chips
  Red cinnamon candies

  Ribbon to decorate

Place popcorn in a very large bowl. In a medium saucepan, combine marshmallows, butter, and milk. Stirring constantly, cook over low heat until marshmallows are melted. Remove from heat and stir in peanut butter, vanilla, and salt. Pour marshmallow mixture over popcorn and stir until evenly coated. Using lightly greased hands, press about ½ cup popcorn mixture into a 4½-inch-long bear-shaped mold. Transfer to waxed paper. Press 2 chocolate chips and 1 candy onto popcorn bear for eyes and nose. Repeat with remaining popcorn mixture, chocolate chips, and candies. Cool completely. Tie ribbon around neck of each bear. Store in an airtight container.

Yield: about 17 popcorn snacks

CRUNCHY PARTY MIX

  2 cups small pretzels
  2 cups chow mein noodles
  2 cups square corn cereal
  1 cup lightly salted roasted peanuts
  1 cup raisins
  3 egg whites
1½ cups granulated sugar
  1 teaspoon ground cinnamon
  1 teaspoon salt
  1 package (14 ounces) candy-
     coated chocolate pieces

Preheat oven to 225 degrees. In a very large bowl, combine pretzels, chow mein noodles, cereal, peanuts, and raisins.

In a medium bowl, beat egg whites until foamy. Stir in sugar, cinnamon, and salt. Pour over pretzel mixture; stir until well coated. Spread evenly on a greased baking sheet. Bake 1 hour, stirring every 15 minutes. Cool completely on pan. Stir in chocolate pieces. Store in an airtight container.

Yield: about 12 cups snack mix

PECAN SHORTBREAD COOKIES

COOKIES

  1 cup butter or margarine, softened
1½ cups granulated sugar
  1 egg
  1 teaspoon vanilla extract
2½ cups all-purpose flour
  1 cup finely ground pecans
  ¼ teaspoon salt

ICING

  5 cups sifted confectioners sugar
  ½ cup milk
  1 teaspoon almond extract
    Green paste food coloring
    Purchased green and red
     decorating icing

Cut in skate and holly shapes and decorated with icing, Pecan Shortbread Cookies have a lightly sweet, nutty flavor.

Continued on page 76

For cookies, trace patterns onto tracing paper; cut out. Preheat oven to 375 degrees. In a large bowl, cream butter and sugar until fluffy. Add egg and vanilla; beat until smooth. In a medium bowl, combine flour, pecans, and salt. Add dry ingredients to creamed mixture; stir until a soft dough forms. Divide dough in half. On a lightly floured surface, use a floured rolling pin to roll out one-half of dough to ⅛-inch thickness. Place 1 pattern on dough and use a sharp knife to cut out cookies. Transfer to a greased baking sheet. Bake 10 to 12 minutes or until edges are light brown. Transfer to a wire rack with waxed paper underneath to cool completely. Repeat for remaining pattern and dough.

For icing, combine sugar, milk, and almond extract in a medium bowl; stir until smooth. Divide icing evenly into 2 bowls. Tint 1 bowl green. Ice holly leaves green and skates white. Allow icing to harden. Transfer purchased decorating icing into separate pastry bags fitted with very small round tips; pipe icing on skate cookies. Use a large round tip to pipe berries on holly cookies. Allow icing to harden. Store in an airtight container.

Yield: about 3½ dozen cookies

SKATING PARTY CAPS

BOY'S CAP

For boy's cap (page 73), you will need a cap, fabric to cover bill, a 2″ x 18″ bias strip of fabric for binding, 14″ of twisted satin cord, paper-backed fusible web, tracing paper, and fabric glue.

1. Use bill as a guide to cut a pattern from tracing paper.
2. Follow manufacturer's instructions to fuse web to wrong side of fabric to cover bill. Use bill pattern to cut bill shape from fabric. Fuse fabric to bill of cap, trimming to fit if necessary.
3. For binding, match wrong sides of bias strip and press in half lengthwise; unfold. Press long raw edges to center; refold binding. Beginning at 1 side of bill, insert edge of bill into fold of binding; glue in place. Trim excess binding. Allow to dry.
4. Beginning ½″ from 1 end of cord, glue cord to base of cap along top of bill, covering raw edges of fabric and binding. Trim remaining end of cord to ½″ from bill. Glue ends to bottom of bill. Allow to dry.

GIRL'S CAP

For girl's cap (page 73), you will need a cap, 20mm paillettes (large round sequins with holes), 5mm sequins, seed beads, thread to match beads, 2 yds each of 1″w satin ribbon and 5/8″w metallic ribbon, beading needle, fabric glue, and florist wire.

1. Bring threaded needle up from wrong side of cap. Thread 1 paillette, 1 sequin, and 1 bead onto needle; bring needle back down through holes in sequin and paillette. Repeat to sew paillettes, sequins, and beads to cap as desired.
2. Glue metallic ribbon along center of satin ribbon; allow to dry. Beginning and ending at front of cap, glue ribbon

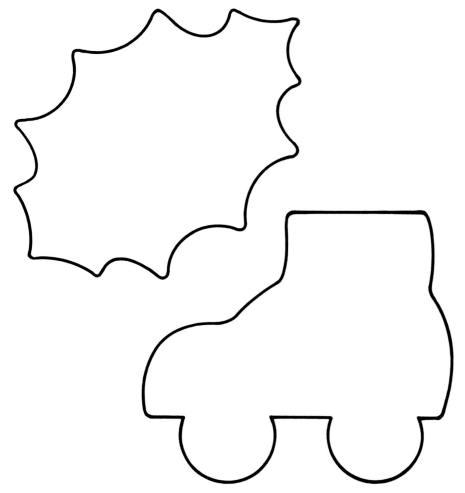

along base of cap, trimming to fit. Form a multi-loop bow from a 33" length of ribbon; wrap bow with wire at center to secure. Knot a 10" length of ribbon around bow center to form bow knot and streamers. Trim ends of streamers. Glue bow to front of cap. Allow to dry.

FAVOR BAGS

For each bag (page 73), you will need a 7" x 20" piece of clear cellophane, transparent tape, a 6" square each of poster board and wrapping paper, white paper, curling ribbon, spray adhesive, hole punch, and a "Beary" Christmas Popcorn Snack (page 74).

1. Match short edges of cellophane piece and fold in half; crease fold (bottom of bag).
2. To tape side edges of bag together, cut two 10" pieces of tape. Center 1 piece of tape on 1 side edge of cellophane piece and press in place; fold tape over edges of cellophane and press in place. Repeat for remaining side edge.
3. To form bottom of bag, match 1 side of bag to fold line at bottom of bag, forming a point (Fig 1). Fold point 1½" toward bottom of bag and tape to secure. Repeat for remaining side.

Fig. 1

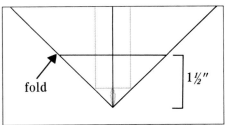

4. For bag liner, use spray adhesive to glue poster board to wrong side of wrapping paper. Cut a 3" x 4" piece

from covered poster board. Place in bottom of bag. Set aside remaining covered poster board.
5. Place popcorn snack in bag.
6. Tie lengths of ribbon together into a bow around top of bag and curl ends.
7. For tag, cut a ¾" x 2¼" tag shape from white paper. Write name on tag. Use spray adhesive to glue tag to remaining piece of covered poster board. Trim poster board to ⅛" from tag. Punch hole in tag; thread tag onto ribbon.

SKATING PARTY INVITATIONS

For each invitation (page 74), you will need a 6¼" x 9" piece of heavy white paper for invitation, a 5" x 6" piece of plain white paper for skate, gold and printed foil wrapping paper, two 1½" dia. wooden circle cutouts, metallic acrylic paint, foam brush, ½ yd of 1/16" dia. metallic cord, large needle, a 1" white pom-pom, red felt-tip pen with fine point, tracing paper, spray adhesive, and craft glue.

1. Use spray adhesive to glue 6¼" x 9" paper piece to wrong side of printed wrapping paper; trim printed paper even with white paper. Matching short edges, fold in half with printed paper side out.
2. For skate, use a pencil to trace solid lines and dots of pattern onto 5" x 6" paper piece. Use pen to trace dashed lines onto paper. Cut out skate.
3. With skate centered and top of skate ⅜" from fold, use spray adhesive to glue skate to invitation.
4. For lacing, use needle to punch a hole through front of invitation at each dot on skate. Thread needle with cord and lace through holes in invitation using method used to lace shoes. Tie ends into a bow; knot and trim ends.
5. For wheels, paint wooden cutouts; allow to dry. Trace star pattern onto tracing paper; cut out. Use pattern to cut 2 stars from gold wrapping paper. Use spray adhesive to glue 1 star to each wheel.
6. Use craft glue to glue wheels and pom-pom to skate.

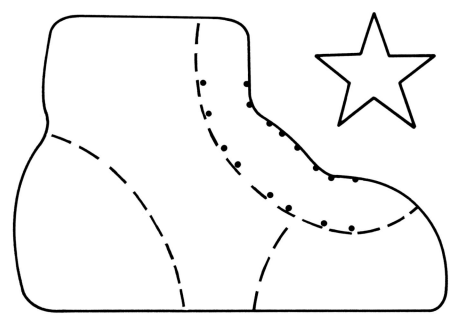

CHRISTMAS PICNIC

Festive red and green watermelons are a natural decorating choice for this indoor Christmas picnic. Watermelon slices and whimsical Santas fashioned from paper plates, along with cheery red and white table linens, add fresh country charm to the gathering. Guests can begin with appetizers and soup, then carry individual picnic baskets over to the fireside to dine on cozy quilts. Our Southern-style menu is perfect for this informal party.

Shrimp Pâté

Artichoke-Brie Spread

Spicy Tomato Soup

Peppered Black-Eyed Pea Salad

Oven-Fried Catfish Sandwiches

Chocolate Chip-Mocha Bars

Chocolate-Pecan Cookies

Fireside Punch

FIRESIDE PUNCH

6 cups apple cider
1 can (12 ounces) frozen lemonade
   concentrate
1 cup granulated sugar
1 cup peach schnapps
1 cup rum
   Fresh lemon peel to garnish

In a Dutch oven, combine first
3 ingredients; bring to a boil. Remove
from heat; stir in schnapps and rum.
Serve hot in mugs and garnish with
lemon peel.

Yield: about twelve 6-ounce servings

SHRIMP PÂTÉ

1 package (8 ounces) cream cheese,
   softened
8 ounces shrimp, cooked, peeled,
   and deveined
1 cup (4 ounces) shredded Cheddar
   cheese
3 tablespoons Dijon-style mustard
2 teaspoons prepared horseradish
½ teaspoon dried dill weed
½ teaspoon garlic powder
½ teaspoon salt
¼ teaspoon ground black pepper
¼ teaspoon onion powder
3 large cucumbers, thinly sliced
   Sweet red pepper and
      fresh parsley to garnish

In a blender or food processor,
process first 10 ingredients until shrimp
are finely chopped. Cover and
refrigerate until well chilled. Shape into
½-inch balls and place on cucumber
slices.

For garnish, use a star-shaped aspic
cutter to cut out stars from red pepper;
press stars and parsley into pâté. Store
in an airtight container in refrigerator.

Yield: about 9 dozen appetizers

*Packed in little jars, Peppered Black-Eyed Pea Salad is bursting with
country flavor. Shown on previous page: Bites of Shrimp Pâté are topped
with sweet pepper stars and served on cucumber slices, and warm Fireside
Punch is delightfully fruity.*

PEPPERED BLACK-EYED PEA SALAD

¼ cup olive oil
¼ cup apple cider vinegar
2 tablespoons granulated sugar
1 tablespoon garlic powder
2 teaspoons hot pepper sauce
2 teaspoons salt
2 teaspoons ground black pepper
½ teaspoon ground ginger
4 cans (15 ounces each) black-eyed
   peas, drained
2 jars (7 ounces each) pickled baby
   corn, drained and coarsely
   chopped
1 onion, chopped
½ cup finely chopped carrots
¼ cup chopped green pepper
1 jar (2 ounces) chopped pimiento,
   drained

Combine first 8 ingredients in a 1-pint
jar with a tight fitting lid. Shake until
well blended. Refrigerate 8 hours or
overnight to allow flavors to blend.

In a large bowl, combine peas, corn,
onion, carrots, green pepper, and
pimiento. Pour dressing over vegetables
and stir until well coated. Refrigerate
until ready to serve. Serve chilled.

Yield: about 8 servings

Attractively garnished with sour cream and fresh parsley, Spicy Tomato Soup can be served in bowls or mugs. Red pepper and a variety of herbs give the soup a distinctive flavor. Creamy, cheesy Artichoke-Brie Spread is especially delicious served warm with crackers.

SPICY TOMATO SOUP

- 6 tablespoons butter or margarine
- ½ cup chopped green onions
- 4 cloves garlic, minced
- 3 tablespoons all-purpose flour
- 1½ teaspoons salt
- 1 teaspoon dried tarragon
- ½ teaspoon dried thyme
- ½ teaspoon ground red pepper
- 2 bay leaves
- 6 cups water
- 4 cans (6 ounces each) tomato paste
- 2 cups dry white wine
- 2 cups milk
- 1½ cups whipping cream
  Sour cream and chopped fresh parsley to garnish

In a large stockpot, melt butter over medium heat. Add onions and garlic; cook until onions are tender. Stir in next 6 ingredients; cook 2 minutes.

Whisk in water, tomato paste, wine, milk, and cream. Stirring occasionally, cook 30 minutes or until thickened. Remove bay leaves. For garnish, spoon sour cream into a pastry bag fitted with a small round tip. Ladle soup into bowls, pipe sour cream on soup, and sprinkle parsley over sour cream.

Yield: about thirteen 1-cup servings

ARTICHOKE-BRIE SPREAD

- 2 jars (6 ounces each) marinated artichoke hearts, drained and divided
- 1 package (8 ounces) cream cheese, softened
- 1 cup mayonnaise
- 2 tablespoons chopped green onion
- ½ teaspoon dried oregano leaves, crushed
- ½ teaspoon salt
- ¼ teaspoon ground black pepper
- 2 packages (4½ ounces each) Brie cheese, cut into small pieces
  Fresh parsley to garnish
  Crackers or bread to serve

Preheat oven to 375 degrees. Reserving 1 artichoke heart, coarsely chop remaining artichoke hearts. In a large bowl, combine chopped artichoke hearts, cream cheese, mayonnaise, onion, oregano, salt, and pepper. Stir in Brie cheese. Spoon into a greased 9-inch pie plate. Bake 15 to 20 minutes or until bubbly. For garnish, cut reserved artichoke heart in half. Place artichoke halves and parsley on top of spread. Serve hot with crackers or bread.

Yield: about 3½ cups spread

Served with lettuce, tomato, bacon, and a zesty dressing, Oven-Fried Catfish Sandwiches are a tasty lower-fat version of a Southern favorite.

OVEN-FRIED CATFISH SANDWICHES

8 large sandwich buns
4 catfish fillets (about 1 pound), cut in half crosswise
  Salt and ground black pepper
1½ cups finely crushed corn flake cereal
1 teaspoon paprika
½ teaspoon salt
4 egg whites, beaten until foamy
  Vegetable cooking spray
¾ cup fat-free Thousand Island salad dressing
¼ teaspoon ground red pepper

16 slices bacon, cooked and drained
  Tomato slices
  Lettuce

Wrap buns in aluminum foil; set aside.

Preheat oven to 400 degrees. Sprinkle catfish with salt and black pepper. In a medium bowl, combine cereal crumbs, paprika, and salt. Place egg whites in a shallow bowl. Dip catfish one piece at a time in egg whites and coat with cereal mixture. Place coated pieces of catfish in a baking pan sprayed with cooking spray. Bake 25 to 30 minutes or until catfish is flaky. During last 5 minutes of baking, place buns in oven to heat.

In a small bowl, combine salad dressing and red pepper. Spread salad dressing mixture evenly over both halves of each bun. Place 1 piece of catfish, 2 slices of bacon, tomato, and lettuce on bottom of each bun; replace tops.

Yield: 8 sandwiches

CHOCOLATE CHIP-MOCHA BARS

2 tablespoons instant coffee granules
2 tablespoons hot water
1 box (18.25 ounces) yellow cake mix
1 cup firmly packed brown sugar
½ cup butter or margarine, softened
2 eggs
2 teaspoons vanilla extract
3 cups (one 12-ounce and one 6-ounce package) semisweet chocolate chips, divided

Preheat oven to 350 degrees. In a medium bowl, combine coffee and water. Add cake mix, sugar, butter, eggs, and vanilla to coffee mixture; beat until smooth. Stir in 2 cups chocolate chips. Spoon batter into a greased 9 x 13-inch baking pan. Bake 40 to 45 minutes or until edges begin to pull away from sides of pan. Cool completely in pan. Cut into 1 x 2-inch bars.

Place remaining 1 cup chocolate chips in a disposable pastry bag. Microwave on medium power (50%) for 30 second intervals until melted. Cut the end of the bag to make a small hole. Drizzle chocolate over bars. Allow chocolate to harden. Store in an airtight container.

Yield: about 3 dozen bars

CHOCOLATE-PECAN COOKIES

¾ cup butter or margarine, softened
1 cup firmly packed brown sugar
1 egg yolk
1 teaspoon vanilla extract
1½ cups all-purpose flour
⅓ cup cocoa
1 cup finely chopped pecans
  Pecan halves

Picnickers will love these chocolaty treats! The Chocolate Chip-Mocha Bars have a rich coffee flavor, and Chocolate-Pecan Cookies are chock-full of nuts.

Preheat oven to 350 degrees. In a medium bowl, cream butter and sugar. Beat in egg yolk and vanilla. In a small bowl, combine flour and cocoa. Add dry ingredients to creamed mixture; stir until a soft dough forms. Stir in chopped pecans. Drop heaping teaspoonfuls of dough 1 inch apart onto a greased baking sheet. Press 1 pecan half into each cookie. Bake 8 to 10 minutes or until firm. Transfer to a wire rack to cool completely. Store in an airtight container.

Yield: about 5 dozen cookies

WATERMELON SLICES AND WEDGES

For watermelon slices and wedges (this page), you will need 9″ paper plates (1 plate will make 1 slice or 2 wedges); light green, dark green, red, and dark red acrylic paint; small sponge pieces; pumpkin seeds; black spray paint; and craft glue.

1. (*Note:* To provide stability when painting, place plate on a stack of plates.) Place plate bottom side up.
2. On bottom of plate, use a damp sponge piece to lightly stamp ridged rim of plate with light green paint; allow to dry. Repeat with dark green paint.
3. Leaving approx. ¼″ between colors, use a damp sponge piece to lightly stamp bottom of plate with red paint; allow to dry. Repeat with dark red paint.
4. For slice, fold plate in half with unpainted sides together. For wedges, cut plate in half and fold each half in half with unpainted sides together; glue straight edges of each half together.
5. Spray paint seeds black; allow to dry. Glue seeds to slice or wedge.

WATERMELON SANTAS

For each Santa (this page), you will need a Napkin Tie without ribbons and a Watermelon Slice without seeds (both this page), a paper plate, tracing paper, plastic fork or spoon, hot glue gun, and glue sticks.

1. Glue napkin tie to watermelon slice.
2. Trace mitten pattern, page 122, onto tracing paper; cut out. Use pattern to cut 2 mittens from plate.
3. Glue mittens and fork or spoon to watermelon slice.

For a cute centerpiece, a watering can is filled with greenery and dressed up with a gingham bow and a Watermelon Santa. The paper Watermelon Slices and Wedges make juicy accents, and coordinating Napkin Ties keep plastic cutlery and ticking fabric napkins handy.

NAPKIN TIES

For a set of six napkin ties (this page), you will need 9″ paper plates; light green, dark green, red, and dark red acrylic paint; small sponge pieces; six ½″ red pom-poms; six 1″ white pom-poms; six ¾ yd lengths each of ⅜″w green grosgrain and ¼″w red satin ribbon; black permanent felt-tip pen with fine point; a pink colored pencil; tracing paper; medium weight cardboard; hot glue gun; and glue sticks.

1. Follow Steps 1 - 3 of Watermelon Slices and Wedges instructions, page 84, to paint 1 plate.

2. Place painted plate and 1 plain plate together. Cut plates into six equal wedges.

3. (*Note:* Follow Steps 3 - 10 for each napkin tie.) Cut 1 face piece and 1 hat trim piece from 1 plain paper plate wedge as shown in Fig. 1.

Fig. 1

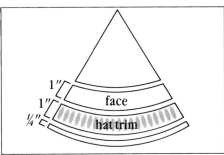

4. For face, glue face piece to painted side of 1 watermelon wedge, matching curves and covering top edge of rind slightly.

5. For mustache, trace mustache pattern, page 122, onto tracing paper; cut out. Use pattern to cut mustache from another plain plate. Glue mustache to painted wedge.

6. Glue 1 red pom-pom to mustache for nose and 1 white pom-pom to top of wedge for pom-pom on hat.

7. Use black pen to draw eyes. Use pink pencil to lightly color cheeks.

8. For hat trim, make cuts between ridges on hat trim piece to ⅛" from top edge. Glue hat trim piece just above eyes, trimming to fit.

9. For backing, cut a wedge from cardboard slightly smaller than Santa. Glue wedge to back of Santa.

10. Glue centers of 1 red and 1 green ribbon length to center back of Santa.

Trimmed with ribbons and a Watermelon Wedge, bright red Picnic Baskets hold sandwiches, cookies, and jars of salad for each guest. The colorful baskets make fun take-home favors, too.

PICNIC BASKET AND PADDED JAR LID

For each basket (this page), you will need a red basket, a Watermelon Wedge (page 84), 1⅜"w red and white gingham craft ribbon, ½"w green grosgrain ribbon, and craft glue.

For each jar lid (page 82), you will need a jar lid with screw ring, fabric for jar lid insert, polyester bonded batting, lightweight cardboard, and craft glue.

1. Glue craft ribbon around basket rim. Glue grosgrain ribbon along center of craft ribbon. Glue watermelon wedge to basket. Allow to dry.

2. For jar lid insert, use flat part of jar lid as a pattern to cut 1 circle each from cardboard, batting, and fabric. Matching edges, glue batting to cardboard. Center fabric circle right side up on batting; glue edge of fabric to batting. Place jar lid insert in screw ring and screw in place over lid.

SOUTHWESTERN ROUNDUP

Celebrate a Southwestern-style Christmas by inviting your favorite cowpokes to mosey on over for a roundup dinner! The spirit of the Old West shines in our centerpiece — there's a little tree nestled in a wooden covered wagon, as well as a cute cactus Santa sporting a cowboy hat and sheriff's badge. Created without sewing, colorful striped table runners double as place mats. Rustic pie pans serve as plate holders, and red bandannas make festive napkins. Featuring Western cuisine, our zesty menu will spice up the evening.

Chili-Cheese Appetizers

Trail Ride Soup

Barbecued Turkey

Mexican Zucchini and Corn

Onion-Cheese Casserole

Buckwheat Rolls

Tex-Mex Chocolate Cake

Chocolate-Rum Coffee

CHILI-CHEESE APPETIZERS

CRUST

- 1½ cups all-purpose flour
- ½ teaspoon chili powder
- ½ teaspoon salt
- ½ cup butter or margarine, cut into small pieces
- ¼ cup cold water

FILLING

- 2 packages (3 ounces each) cream cheese, softened
- ⅓ cup sour cream
- 2 eggs
- 1 teaspoon chili powder
- 1 teaspoon Worcestershire sauce
- ¼ teaspoon salt
- 1 can (4 ounces) chopped green chilies, drained
- 1¼ cups (5 ounces) shredded sharp Cheddar cheese, divided
- Sour cream, prepared salsa, and fresh cilantro to garnish

Preheat oven to 350 degrees. For crust, combine flour, chili powder, and salt in a small bowl. Using a pastry blender or 2 knives, cut in butter until mixture resembles coarse meal. Sprinkle with water; mix until a soft dough forms. Press about ½ tablespoon dough into bottom and up sides of each tin of a greased miniature muffin pan.

For filling, beat cream cheese, sour cream, and eggs until fluffy. Beat in chili powder, Worcestershire sauce, and salt. Stir in chilies and ¾ cup Cheddar cheese. Spoon filling into crusts, filling each full. Sprinkle remaining ½ cup Cheddar cheese evenly over filling. Bake 20 to 25 minutes or until set in center. Remove from pan. Garnish with sour cream, salsa, and cilantro. Serve warm.

Yield: about 3 dozen appetizers

Loaded with fresh vegetables, Trail Ride Soup makes a spicy first course. Shown on previous page: Guests will ask for more of these savory Chili-Cheese Appetizers.

TRAIL RIDE SOUP

- 2 cans (14½ ounces each) chicken broth
- 3 cups tomato juice
- ½ cup chopped fresh cilantro
- 5 tablespoons red wine vinegar
- 2 tablespoons fresh lime juice
- 2 tablespoons olive oil
- 2 teaspoons hot pepper sauce
- 2 teaspoons salt
- 1 teaspoon ground black pepper
- 1 teaspoon granulated sugar
- 1 teaspoon garlic powder
- 1 teaspoon ground cumin seed
- ½ teaspoon celery seed
- 5 large tomatoes (about 2¼ pounds), coarsely chopped
- 1 large cucumber, peeled and coarsely chopped
- 1 green pepper, coarsely chopped
- 1 large onion, coarsely chopped
- 30 corn tortillas, halved to serve
- Sour cream, fresh lime slices, and fresh cilantro to garnish

In a Dutch oven, combine first 13 ingredients. Stirring occasionally, bring to a boil, reduce heat to low, cover, and simmer 30 minutes. In a blender or food processor, process tomatoes, cucumber, green pepper, and onion until finely chopped. Add vegetable mixture to tomato juice mixture and stir until well blended. Cook until heated through. To serve, line each serving bowl with 5 tortilla halves. Ladle soup into bowls. Garnish with sour cream, lime slices, and cilantro.

Yield: 12 servings

Add Southwestern spirit to a traditional holiday entrée with Barbecued Turkey. The homemade sweet-and-spicy sauce is perfect for basting and serving.

BARBECUED TURKEY

2 cups chopped onions
¼ cup vegetable oil
2 cloves garlic, minced
2 cups ketchup
½ cup maple syrup
½ cup water
¼ cup apple cider vinegar
¼ cup molasses
¼ cup Worcestershire sauce
¼ cup Dijon-style mustard
1 teaspoon crushed red pepper
1 teaspoon celery seed
1 teaspoon ground black pepper
½ teaspoon ground ginger
1 turkey (13 to 15 pounds)
2 tablespoons vegetable oil
Salt and ground black pepper

1 cup water
Fresh parsley and red and
    yellow peppers to garnish

For sauce, combine onions, ¼ cup oil, and garlic in a large saucepan. Cook over medium heat until onions are tender. Stir in next 11 ingredients. Bring to a boil, reduce heat to low, and simmer uncovered 30 minutes. Remove from heat.

Preheat oven to 350 degrees. Remove giblets and neck from turkey. Rinse turkey and pat dry. Rub turkey with 2 tablespoons oil. Liberally salt and pepper turkey inside and out. Tie ends of legs to tail with kitchen twine. Place turkey, breast side up, in a large roasting pan. Insert meat thermometer into thickest part of thigh, making sure thermometer does not touch bone. Pour 1 cup water into pan. Baste turkey with sauce. Loosely cover with aluminum foil and roast, basting with sauce every 30 minutes, for 3 to 3½ hours or until meat thermometer registers 180 to 185 degrees and juices run clear when thickest part of thigh is pierced with a fork. Transfer turkey to a serving platter and let stand 20 minutes before carving. Garnish with parsley and peppers. Serve warm sauce with turkey.

Yield: 18 to 20 servings

Sweet red peppers add festive color to flavorful Mexican Zucchini and Corn. Lightly sprinkled with blue cornmeal, old-fashioned Buckwheat Rolls are great warm or cold. The authentic-looking Old-Time Plate Holders are created by "aging" aluminum pie pans. For dining, line the holders with clear plates or glass pie pans.

MEXICAN ZUCCHINI AND CORN

¼ cup butter or margarine
1 teaspoon chili powder
1 teaspoon salt
½ teaspoon garlic powder
½ teaspoon ground cumin seed
2 cans (17 ounces each) whole
    kernel corn, drained
1 pound zucchini, cut into thin
    2-inch-long strips
½ cup chopped sweet red pepper
1 cup (4 ounces) shredded
    Monterey Jack cheese

In a Dutch oven, melt butter over medium heat. Stir in chili powder, salt, garlic powder, and cumin. Add corn, zucchini, and red pepper; cook until zucchini is just tender. Sprinkle cheese over vegetables just before serving.

Yield: about 10 servings

BUCKWHEAT ROLLS

2 packages dry yeast
½ cup warm water
1¼ cups buckwheat groats
½ cup old-fashioned rolled oats
¼ cup firmly packed brown sugar
¼ cup butter or margarine, melted
1 tablespoon salt
1¾ cups boiling water
4 cups bread flour, divided
    Vegetable cooking spray
⅛ cup blue cornmeal

In a small bowl, dissolve yeast in ½ cup warm water. In a large bowl, combine buckwheat, oats, sugar, butter, salt, and 1¾ cups boiling water; let stand 10 minutes. Stir in yeast mixture and 1 cup flour. Gradually add remaining flour; stir until a soft dough forms. Turn onto a lightly floured surface and knead until dough becomes smooth and elastic. Place in a large bowl sprayed with cooking spray, turning once to coat top of dough.

Cover and let rise in a warm place (80 to 85 degrees) 1½ to 2 hours or until doubled in size. Turn dough onto a lightly floured surface and punch down. Shape dough into 2-inch balls and place 2 inches apart on a greased baking sheet. Using a serrated knife, make decorative cuts ¼-inch-deep in tops of rolls. Spray tops of rolls with cooking spray, sprinkle with cornmeal, cover, and let rise in a warm place 1 hour or until doubled in size.

Preheat oven to 400 degrees. Bake 18 to 20 minutes or until golden brown. Serve warm.

Yield: about 2½ dozen rolls

ONION-CHEESE CASSEROLE

2 cups finely crushed butter-
    flavored crackers (about
    45 crackers), divided
½ cup butter or margarine, divided
3 pounds onions, thinly sliced
2 tablespoons all-purpose flour
½ teaspoon salt
½ teaspoon ground black pepper
2 cups milk
½ pound pasteurized process
    cheese, cut into small pieces
    Sweet red pepper, cut into rings
    and fresh jalapeño pepper to
    garnish

Preheat oven to 350 degrees. Spread 1 cup cracker crumbs in a greased 8 x 11-inch baking dish. In a large skillet, melt ¼ cup butter over medium heat. Add onions; cook until tender. Spoon onions over cracker crumbs.

In same skillet, melt remaining ¼ cup butter over medium-high heat. Stir in flour, salt, and pepper; cook 1 minute. Gradually stir in milk. Stirring constantly, cook until thickened. Add cheese and stir until

Sweet onions and mellow cheese are combined to create this deliciously buttery Onion-Cheese Casserole.

smooth. Pour cheese mixture over onions. Sprinkle remaining 1 cup cracker crumbs over cheese mixture. Bake 25 to 30 minutes or until lightly browned. Garnish with red pepper rings and jalapeño pepper.

Yield: about 12 servings

Ground black pepper is the secret ingredient in the rich, cinnamon-spiced Tex-Mex Chocolate Cake. Cups of creamy Chocolate-Rum Coffee are garnished with cinnamon sticks.

TEX-MEX CHOCOLATE CAKE

CAKE
- 1½ cups all-purpose flour
- 1¼ cups granulated sugar
- 3 tablespoons cocoa
- 2 teaspoons baking soda
- 1 teaspoon ground black pepper
- 1 teaspoon ground cinnamon
- ½ teaspoon salt
- 4 eggs
- ½ cup milk
- ½ cup coffee-flavored liqueur
- ⅓ cup vegetable oil
- 1 tablespoon white vinegar
- 1 teaspoon vanilla extract
- 2 packages (3 ounces each) cream cheese, softened
- 1 package (6 ounces) semisweet chocolate chips, melted

FROSTING
- 6 cups sifted confectioners sugar
- ⅓ cup cocoa
- 1½ cups butter or margarine, softened
- 2 tablespoons milk
- 1 tablespoon vanilla extract

  Conchas with suede trim to decorate

For cake, preheat oven to 350 degrees. In a large bowl, sift flour, sugar, cocoa, baking soda, pepper, cinnamon, and salt. In a medium bowl, whisk next 6 ingredients. Add egg mixture to dry ingredients; stir until well blended.

In a medium bowl, beat cream cheese and chocolate until well blended. Beat cream cheese mixture into batter. Pour batter into 2 greased and floured 9-inch round cake pans. Bake 30 to 35 minutes or until a toothpick inserted in center of cake comes out clean. Cool in pans 10 minutes; remove from pans and cool completely on a wire rack.

For frosting, combine sugar and cocoa in a large bowl. Add remaining ingredients; beat until smooth. Frost between layers, sides, and top of cake. Spoon remaining frosting into a pastry bag fitted with a large star tip. Pipe frosting on top and along bottom edge of cake. Use a small amount of frosting to attach conchas to sides of cake. Store in an airtight container in refrigerator.

Yield: about 16 servings

CHOCOLATE-RUM COFFEE

2 quarts brewed coffee
3 cans (12 ounces each) evaporated milk
1 can (16 ounces) chocolate syrup
½ cup firmly packed brown sugar
1 cup rum
  Cinnamon sticks to garnish

In a Dutch oven, combine coffee, milk, chocolate syrup, and brown sugar. Stirring occasionally, cook over medium-high heat until sugar dissolves and mixture begins to boil; remove from heat. Stir in rum. Pour into mugs and garnish with cinnamon sticks.

Yield: about twenty 6-ounce servings

ROUNDUP CENTERPIECE

This unique centerpiece (pages 86 and 87) will add lively Western flair to your party. Our Cactus Santa (this page) made from an artificial cactus is easy to assemble. From the cactus to the craft mop, everything you need to make the Santa is available at most craft stores.

More holiday spirit is added to the scene with our 18" high tree. We placed the tree in a 3½" high metal bucket filled with plastic foam and covered the foam with sheet moss. For a colorful accent, 5" strips of bandanna fabric were tied to the branches of the tree. A length of ¼" dia. rope was used for garland around the tree and then looped around other pieces of the table setting. For ornaments, we threaded strips of 3" long synthetic suede fringe (available at fabric stores) through 1½" dia. conchas and then glued the conchas to the rope garland. Our tree topper is an "aged" sheriff's badge — a party favor that has been lightly sprayed with grey and black spray paint.

Miniature wired greenery garland spruces up the purchased 13" high wooden covered wagon that completes our centerpiece. The small wreath on the wagon is made from a loop of the garland and brightened by a bow tied from a strip of bandanna fabric.

CACTUS SANTA

For Santa (page 87), you will need a 16" high artificial cactus, an 18" square of fabric for bandanna, an 8" long unbleached cotton craft mop, a 10mm red bead for nose, two 5mm black beads for eyes, sheriff's badge party favor, grey and black spray paint, a purchased cowboy hat to fit cactus, 15" of ⅛" dia. silver cord, hot glue gun, and glue sticks.

1. For bandanna, fold fabric square in half diagonally. Tie bandanna around "neck" of cactus. Glue in place if necessary.
2. For beard, cut a 2½"w section from craft mop; trim to desired length (we trimmed ours to 3" long). Glue beard to cactus above bandanna. For mustache, cut several strands from remaining mop and twist together. Knot a separate mop strand around center of mustache and glue mustache to cactus above beard.
3. Glue red bead to mustache for nose and black beads to cactus for eyes.
4. To "age" badge, lightly spray with grey, then black, paint. Allow to dry. Glue badge to bandanna.
5. Knot silver cord around crown of hat. Place hat on cactus.

WESTERN TABLE RUNNERS

For each runner (pages 86 and 87), you will need fabric, 3" long synthetic suede fringe (available at fabric stores), and ⅝"w paper-backed fusible web.

1. Cut fabric ⅝" larger on all sides than desired finished size of table runner.
2. To hem long edges, cut 2 web lengths same length as 1 long edge of fabric. Follow manufacturer's instructions to fuse 1 web length along each long edge on wrong side of fabric. Remove paper backing. Fold each long edge of fabric ⅝" to wrong side; fuse in place.
3. For fringe, cut 2 web lengths and 2 fringe lengths same length as 1 short edge of runner. Fuse 1 web length along each short edge on right side of fabric. Remove paper backing. Place 1 fringe length along 1 short edge of runner and fuse in place. Repeat for remaining short edge.

OLD-TIME PLATE HOLDERS

For each plate holder (page 90), you will need an aluminum pie pan; a hammer, awl, and screwdriver; muriatic acid (available at hardware stores); a plastic bucket large enough to hold pie pan; tongs; rubber gloves; and paper towels.

Note: Plate holders are for decorative use only. Place clear glass or paper plates in holders before using.

1. Use hammer, awl, and screwdriver to distress pan.
2. (*Note:* Muriatic acid is used to remove shiny surface from pan. Follow manufacturer's instructions and practice caution when using acid; wear rubber gloves and work in a well ventilated area.) Pour acid into bucket to a depth of approx. 2". Fill remainder of bucket with water. Using tongs, place pan into acid for several minutes; when surface of pan begins to bubble, remove from acid and rinse well with water. Place pan on paper towels and pat dry.

HOLIDAY BEACH PARTY

'Tis the "sea-sun" to be jolly, so turn up the heat and throw an indoor beach bash! Guests are greeted with leis and ushered into an island paradise where handmade starfish Santas play volleyball at a little net. Colorful beach toys are scattered among a jungle of tropical houseplants, and a child's float ring is transformed into a clever wreath. A beach towel serves as a table runner. Frisbees® make cute plates, and sunglasses trimmed with starfish Santas or palm trees double as napkin rings and party favors. Our luau-style menu will make the party a sunny success.

Crab au Gratin
Cheddar Crackers
Seafood Shish Kabobs
Pineapple Rice
Grilled Red Onions
Coconut Bread
Piña Colada Cake
Pineapple Wine Coolers

94

PINEAPPLE WINE COOLERS

1 quart pineapple juice
1 bottle (750 ml) dry white wine
1 cup vodka
1 cup granulated sugar
   Pineapple chunks and maraschino cherries with stems on wooden skewers to garnish

In a 2½-quart container, combine first 4 ingredients; stir until sugar dissolves. Chill; serve over ice. Garnish with pineapple and cherries.

Yield: about ten 6-ounce servings

CHEDDAR CRACKERS

1 cup butter or margarine, melted
1 cup (4 ounces) shredded sharp Cheddar cheese
1 tablespoon dried minced onion
1 teaspoon steak sauce
2½ cups all-purpose flour
1 teaspoon salt
¼ teaspoon ground red pepper

Trace seashell pattern onto tracing paper; cut out. Preheat oven to 350 degrees. In a large bowl, beat first 4 ingredients until well blended. Add remaining ingredients; stir until a soft dough forms. On a lightly floured surface, use a floured rolling pin to roll out dough to ¼-inch thickness. Place pattern on dough and use a sharp knife to cut out crackers. Bake on a greased baking sheet 22 to 25 minutes or until light brown. Cool completely.

Yield: about 1½ dozen crackers

CRAB AU GRATIN

2 tablespoons cornstarch
2 tablespoons water
1½ cups milk
¼ pound pasteurized process cheese
2 egg yolks

Scallop shells make fun serving dishes for creamy Crab au Gratin, and the seashell shape is also reflected in the crispy Cheddar Crackers. Featuring a beach scene, the easy-to-make Beach Party Invitations provide details. Shown on previous page: Pineapple Wine Coolers are light and fruity.

½ teaspoon salt
¼ teaspoon ground black pepper
⅛ teaspoon ground red pepper
1½ pounds lump crabmeat
   Paprika and fresh parsley to garnish

In a small bowl, combine cornstarch and water. In a medium saucepan, combine next 6 ingredients. Stirring constantly, cook over medium heat until mixture boils; add cornstarch mixture and cook until thickened. Stir in crabmeat. Spoon into 5-inch seashells. Garnish with paprika and parsley.

Yield: about 6 servings

PINEAPPLE RICE

3 tablespoons butter or margarine
3 tablespoons sesame oil
1 cup chopped onion
4 cans (14½ ounces each) chicken broth
3 cups uncooked brown rice
1 teaspoon salt
½ teaspoon ground black pepper
1 can (15¼ ounces) pineapple tidbits, drained
¼ cup finely chopped green pepper
¼ cup finely chopped sweet red pepper

In a Dutch oven over medium heat, combine butter and oil. Add onion and cook until onion is tender. Add broth,

Served atop a bed of Pineapple Rice, Seafood Shish Kabobs feature alternating bites of shrimp, swordfish, salmon, peppers, and onion. A tangy-sweet sauce is perfect for dipping the savory morsels.

rice, salt, and pepper. Bring to a boil, reduce heat, cover, and simmer 50 to 60 minutes or until all liquid is absorbed. Stir in remaining ingredients; cook 2 minutes longer.

Yield: about 10 servings

SEAFOOD SHISH KABOBS

KABOBS

1 pound large shrimp, peeled and deveined
1 pound *each* swordfish and salmon (skin and bones removed), cut into pieces
1 cup vegetable oil
½ cup soy sauce
3 tablespoons honey
4 cloves garlic, minced
2 teaspoons ground ginger
½ teaspoon ground black pepper

1 green pepper, cut into pieces
1 sweet red pepper, cut into pieces
1 red onion, cut into pieces

SAUCE
2 cups firmly packed brown sugar
⅓ cup cornstarch
1⅓ cups red wine vinegar
1⅓ cups pineapple juice
1 cup finely chopped green pepper
½ cup finely chopped sweet red pepper
¼ cup soy sauce
1 teaspoon garlic powder
1 teaspoon ground ginger
Fresh lemon slices to serve

For kabobs, place shrimp, swordfish, and salmon in separate resealable plastic bags. Combine next 6 ingredients in a medium bowl. Pour ⅓ of oil mixture

into each bag and seal. Refrigerate 8 hours or overnight.

Preheat oven to 350 degrees. Reserving marinade, alternate pieces of seafood, peppers, and onion on 8 metal skewers. Place kabobs on a rack in a roasting pan. Basting with reserved marinade and turning every 10 minutes, bake 20 to 25 minutes or until fish flakes with a fork.

For sauce, combine sugar and cornstarch in a medium saucepan. Stir in next 7 ingredients. Stirring constantly, bring to a boil and cook until thickened. Serve kabobs with warm sauce and lemon slices.

Yield: 8 servings

GRILLED RED ONIONS

- 4 large red onions, cut crosswise into ½-inch slices
- 1 cup red wine vinegar
- 1 cup soy sauce
- 1 cup honey
- 2 teaspoons garlic powder
- 1 teaspoon ground black pepper
- ¼ cup vegetable oil

Place onions in a 1-gallon resealable plastic bag. In a medium bowl, whisk next 5 ingredients. Pour vinegar mixture into bag and seal. Refrigerate 8 hours or overnight.

Heat oil in a large skillet over medium-high heat. Using a slotted spoon, place onions in skillet and cook until brown on both sides; drain on paper towels. Serve warm.

Yield: about 8 servings

COCONUT BREAD

- 2 packages dry yeast
- ¼ cup warm water
- 3 cups bread flour
- 1½ cups sweetened shredded coconut, toasted
- ¼ cup nonfat dry milk
- ¼ cup granulated sugar
- ½ teaspoon salt
- ½ cup pineapple juice, warmed
- ¼ cup butter or margarine, melted
- 1 egg
  Vegetable cooking spray

In a small bowl, dissolve yeast in water. In a large bowl, combine flour, toasted coconut, dry milk, sugar, and salt. Add yeast mixture, pineapple juice, butter, and egg; stir until a soft dough forms. Turn onto a lightly floured surface and knead 5 minutes or until dough becomes smooth and elastic. Place in a large bowl sprayed with

A special marinade makes Grilled Red Onions a tasty treat, and richly textured Coconut Bread has a delightful flavor. The cute Starfish Santas are easy to make from paper or crafting foam.

cooking spray, turning once to coat top of dough. Cover and let rise in a warm place (80 to 85 degrees) 1 hour or until doubled in size. Turn dough onto a lightly floured surface and punch down. Shape dough into a loaf and place in a greased 5 x 9-inch loaf pan. Spray top of dough with cooking spray, cover,

and let rise in a warm place 1 hour or until doubled in size.

Preheat oven to 375 degrees. Bake 35 to 40 minutes or until bread is golden brown and sounds hollow when tapped. Serve warm.

Yield: 1 loaf bread

Shaped like one of the Starfish Santas, this delectable Piña Colada Cake is sprinkled with brown sugar "sand" and decorated with a pair of "holly" Palm Tree Sunglasses. The cute Souvenir Photo Frames can display shots from the party for take-home favors (you'll want to have an instant camera on hand to capture the fun!).

PIÑA COLADA CAKE

CAKE
- 1 cup firmly packed brown sugar to decorate
- 1 box (18.25 ounces) yellow cake mix
- 3 eggs
- 1⅓ cups piña colada drink mixer
- ⅓ cup vegetable oil
- 1½ cups sweetened shredded coconut, toasted

FROSTING
- 4 cups sifted confectioners sugar
- ½ cup vegetable shortening
- ½ cup butter or margarine, softened
- 2 tablespoons milk
- 1 tablespoon vanilla extract
  Red and brown paste food coloring

Decorated sunglasses with ear pieces removed (see Palm Tree Sunglasses, page 101) and red glass ball ornament to decorate

To make "sand" to decorate cake, spread brown sugar on an ungreased baking sheet, loosely cover, and allow to dry 8 hours or overnight.

For cake, preheat oven to 350 degrees. In a large bowl, combine cake mix, eggs, drink mixer, and oil. Mix according to package instructions. Stir in toasted coconut. Pour batter into a greased and floured 12½-inch-wide star-shaped baking pan. Bake 40 to 45 minutes or until a toothpick inserted in center of cake comes out clean. Cool in pan 10 minutes. Remove from pan and cool completely on a wire rack.

For frosting, combine sugar, shortening, butter, milk, and vanilla in a large bowl; beat until smooth. Spoon ½ cup frosting into a pastry bag fitted with a large star tip. Spoon ½ cup frosting into each of 2 small bowls; tint red and tan. Spoon tan frosting into a pastry bag fitted with a small round tip. Spread red frosting over top and sides of 1 tip of cake for hat. Spread white frosting over top and sides of remainder of cake. Referring to photo, pipe tan frosting on cake and sprinkle brown sugar over top of cake. Pipe white frosting on cake for hat trim and pompom. Place sunglasses and ornament on cake. Remove sunglasses and ornament before serving.

Yield: about 16 servings

BEACH PARTY INVITATIONS

For each invitation (page 96), you will need white, yellow, red, green, and brown card stock paper; Design Master® glossy wood tone spray (available at craft stores or florist shops); tracing paper; ⅛" hole punch; and craft glue.

1. Cut a 4¼" x 6¼" piece of yellow paper and a 4" x 5¼" piece of white paper.
2. Center and glue white paper to yellow paper.
3. Lightly spray another piece of white paper with wood tone spray. Allow to dry.
4. Trace beach, small tree trunk, and small leaf patterns, this page, onto tracing paper; cut out.
5. Use patterns to cut 1 beach from sprayed white paper, 2 tree trunks from brown paper, and 6 leaves from green paper. Use hole punch to cut 6 circles from red paper.
6. Matching bottom edges, glue beach to invitation. Glue 1 trunk to each side of beach. Glue 3 leaves to top of each trunk to resemble palm trees. Glue 3 red circles to center of leaves on each tree.

SOUVENIR PHOTO FRAME

For a frame to hold a Polaroid® photograph (page 99), you will need white, yellow, red, blue, green, and brown card stock paper; ¼" hole punch; Design Master® glossy wood tone spray (available at craft stores and florist shops); tracing paper; 1 small Starfish Santa (page 101); craft knife; and craft glue.

1. For frame front, cut a 4" x 6" piece of blue paper. Use craft knife to cut a 2¾" square from center of paper as shown in Fig. 1.

Fig. 1

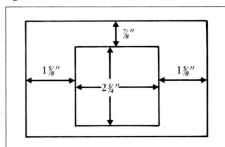

2. Lightly spray white paper with wood tone spray. Allow to dry.
3. Trace beach, large tree trunk, and large leaf patterns, this page, onto tracing paper; cut out.
4. Use patterns to cut 1 beach from sprayed white paper, 2 tree trunks from brown paper, and 6 leaves from green paper. Use hole punch to cut 6 circles from red paper.
5. Matching bottom edges, center and glue beach to frame front; trim sides to fit. Glue 1 trunk to each side of beach. Glue 3 leaves to top of each trunk to resemble palm trees. Glue 3 red circles to center of leaves on each tree. Glue starfish Santa to beach.
6. For frame back, cut a 4¼" x 6¼" piece of yellow paper. Center frame front on frame back and glue side and bottom edges only of frame front to frame back.
7. Trim ¾" from bottom edge of photograph and insert into top of frame.

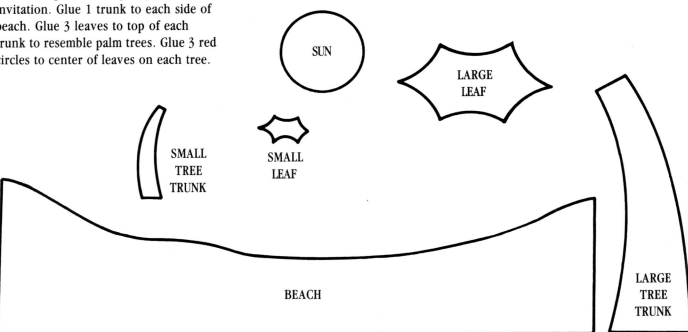

STARFISH SANTAS

For each Starfish Santa (pages 94 and 95), you will need white and red card stock paper or $1/16$" thick crafting foam; Design Master® glossy wood tone spray (available at craft stores and florist shops); a brown permanent felt-tip pen with fine point; tracing paper; craft glue; small sharp scissors or craft knife (for cutting foam); $1/4$" hole punch; $1/8$" hole punch (small Starfish Santa only); a $3/8$" white pom-pom and a $1/2$" red bead (medium Starfish Santa only); and a $1/2$" white pom-pom, $1^1/2$"w miniature sunglasses (available at craft stores), and a $1/2$" red bead (all optional; large Starfish Santa only).

1. Trace desired size starfish Santa, hat, and hat trim patterns, page 120 or 121, onto tracing paper; cut out.
2. Use patterns to cut starfish Santa and hat trim from white paper or foam and hat from red paper or foam.
3. Spraying a heavier coat along edges, lightly spray starfish Santa with wood tone spray; allow to dry.
4. Glue hat and hat trim to starfish Santa.
5. For small starfish Santa, use $1/4$" hole punch to cut 1 circle from white paper or foam and glue to top of hat. For medium starfish Santa, glue $3/8$" pom-pom to top of hat. For large starfish Santa, glue $1/2$" pom-pom to top of hat or trace pom-pom pattern, page 121, onto tracing paper; cut out. Use pattern to cut 1 pom-pom from paper or foam and glue to top of hat.
6. For nose on small starfish Santa, use $1/8$" hole punch to cut 1 circle from red paper or foam and glue to center of starfish Santa. For nose on medium or large starfish Santa, glue red bead to center of starfish Santa or use $1/4$" hole punch to cut 1 circle from red paper or foam and glue to center of starfish Santa.
7. Use pen to draw eyes and a line along center of each arm and leg. If desired, glue miniature sunglasses to large starfish Santa.

PALM TREE AND STARFISH SANTA SUNGLASSES

For each pair of sunglasses, you will need a pair of sunglasses, hot glue gun, and glue sticks.
For Palm Tree Sunglasses (page 99), you will also need yellow, brown, green, and red $1/16$" thick crafting foam; tracing paper; $1/8$" hole punch; small sharp scissors or craft knife (for cutting foam); and craft glue.
For Starfish Santa Sunglasses (page 95), you will also need 2 small Starfish Santas made from crafting foam (this page).

PALM TREE SUNGLASSES

1. Trace sun, small tree trunk, and small leaf patterns, page 100, onto tracing paper; cut out.
2. Use patterns to cut 2 suns from yellow foam, 2 tree trunks from brown foam, and 6 leaves from green foam. Use hole punch to cut 6 circles from red foam.
3. Use craft glue to glue leaves and tree trunks to suns to resemble palm trees; glue 3 red circles to center of leaves on each tree. Allow to dry.
4. Hot glue decorations to rims of sunglasses.

STARFISH SANTA SUNGLASSES
Hot glue starfish Santas to rims of sunglasses.

"SEA-SUN"-AL WREATH

A 17" dia. child's float ring becomes a colorful wreath (page 94) when a few beach party accessories are added. We began by securing lengths of artificial greenery along the bottom of the float ring with $1/2$" dia. nylon rope. We used a bright felt-tip marker to write a seasonal message on a coordinating piece of poster board cut to fit in the scoop of a $16^1/2$" plastic sand shovel. We hot glued the poster board to the shovel and then attached the shovel and another length of knotted rope to the wreath with nylon line. A pair of large Starfish Santas (this page) and a few seashells were hot glued to the shovel and rope. A 22" length of $1/16$"w satin ribbon tied around the top of the ring makes a hanging loop for the cheery wreath.

SUNNY CENTERPIECE

Recreate a fun day at the beach by using bright beach toys for centerpiece decorations.

The focus of the scene (pages 94 and 95) is a miniature volleyball net — just right for summer fun! We created the net by placing two painted 15" long wooden dowels into two 7" dia. lawn mower wheels. A length cut from a 6" high table tennis net (we found ours at a sporting goods store) was hot glued to the dowels. Glued to the net is a pair of Starfish Santas (this page), ready to spike the next ball.

"Palm" trees were created by placing tropical house plants in inexpensive colored plastic tumblers and surrounding them with aquarium gravel.

A beach towel becomes a table runner, and Frisbees® make the festive plates that complete this sunny scene.

Down-Home Get-Together

This year, celebrate Christmas with a casual get-together down on the farm! Your dining room can be transformed into a miniature barnyard complete with haystacks, farm animals crafted from egg shapes, and a barn topped with patchwork scraps. A tabletop tree is trimmed with baskets, bells, and screen bows, and place mats are painted with cow spots. After the holidays, these cute creations will be right at home beside your other country collectibles! To complement the friendly setting, our menu features hearty country cooking.

Cream Cheese Deviled Eggs

Honey-Baked Ham

Green Beans and New Potatoes

Corn Bread Salad

Cracklin' Biscuits

Peach-Apple Cobbler with Whipped Cinnamon Sauce

HONEY-BAKED HAM

- 5 to 6 pound fully cooked semi-boneless ham
- 1½ cups apple cider
- 1½ cups honey, divided
- ¼ cup soy sauce
- 3 tablespoons cornstarch
- 3 tablespoons water

Preheat oven to 450 degrees. Place ham in a large roasting pan. Bake 30 minutes or until outside is crisp. Remove from oven. Reduce oven temperature to 325 degrees.

In a large bowl, combine cider, 1 cup honey, and soy sauce; pour over ham. Cover and bake 2 to 3 hours or until a meat thermometer registers 140 degrees, basting ham frequently with cider mixture. Reserve drippings.

For sauce, combine cornstarch and water in a small bowl; stir until smooth. In a medium saucepan, combine reserved meat drippings and remaining ½ cup honey; bring to a boil. Stirring constantly, add cornstarch mixture, bring to a boil, and cook until thickened. Serve warm sauce with ham.

Yield: 10 to 12 servings

GREEN BEANS AND NEW POTATOES

- 2 pounds fresh green beans
- 2 pounds unpeeled new potatoes, quartered
- 10 slices bacon
- 1 onion, chopped
- 2 cloves garlic, minced
- ½ cup chopped fresh parsley
- ¼ cup apple cider vinegar
- 2 teaspoons dried oregano leaves
- 1 teaspoon salt
- ½ teaspoon ground black pepper

Honey-Baked Ham is served with a sweet, tangy sauce, and Green Beans and New Potatoes are a country favorite. The chilled Corn Bread Salad is a delicious mixture of down-home flavors. Friendly Farm Animals keep watch over the dinner table, and the spotted Country Place Mats are easy to make.

Wash beans, trim ends, and remove strings. Cut into 1½-inch pieces. In a Dutch oven, combine green beans and potatoes. Cover with salted water and bring to a boil. Cover and cook until potatoes are tender; drain in a colander.

In a large skillet, cook bacon until crisp. Drain on paper towels; crumble.

Add onion and garlic to bacon drippings; cook until onion is tender. Stir in green beans and potatoes, parsley, vinegar, oregano, salt, and pepper. Stirring occasionally, cook until edges of potatoes begin to brown. Stir in crumbled bacon.

Yield: about 12 servings

CREAM CHEESE DEVILED EGGS

9 hard-cooked eggs, shelled
1 package (3 ounces) cream cheese, softened
½ cup (2 ounces) finely shredded Cheddar cheese
¼ cup sour cream
¼ cup finely chopped celery
1 tablespoon finely chopped fresh parsley
½ teaspoon Dijon-style mustard
½ teaspoon salt
½ teaspoon ground black pepper

Fresh parsley and paprika to garnish

Cut eggs in half lengthwise. Reserving whites, remove yolks and place in a blender or food processor. Add next 8 ingredients; process until well blended. Spoon yolk mixture into a pastry bag fitted with a large star tip; pipe into egg white halves. Garnish with parsley and paprika. Store in an airtight container in refrigerator.

Yield: 1½ dozen deviled eggs

CORN BREAD SALAD

6 cups crumbled corn bread
1 pound bacon, cooked, drained, and crumbled
2 cups (8 ounces) shredded Cheddar cheese
2 large tomatoes, chopped
1 can (17 ounces) whole kernel corn, drained
1 cup mayonnaise
½ cup chopped green onions
½ cup chopped green pepper

In a large bowl, combine all ingredients. Cover and refrigerate until well chilled.

Yield: about 12 servings

Cream Cheese Deviled Eggs feature a blend of Cheddar and cream cheeses with crunchy bits of celery. Cheddar cheese and crispy bits of pork make the hearty Cracklin' Biscuits especially tasty.

CRACKLIN' BISCUITS

8 ounces salt pork, diced
1 package dry yeast
¼ cup warm water
2 cups buttermilk biscuit mix
2 cups (8 ounces) shredded Cheddar cheese
⅔ cup warm milk
½ cup dried minced onions

Cook salt pork in a medium skillet over medium-high heat until crisp and golden brown. Transfer salt pork to paper towels to drain.

Preheat oven to 450 degrees. In a small bowl, dissolve yeast in water; let stand 10 minutes. In a medium bowl, combine biscuit mix, cheese, milk, onions, salt pork, and yeast mixture; stir until a soft dough forms. On a lightly floured surface, use a floured rolling pin to roll out dough to ½-inch thickness. Use a 2½-inch biscuit cutter to cut out biscuits. Transfer to a greased baking sheet. Bake 10 to 12 minutes or until light brown. Serve warm.

Yield: about 1 dozen biscuits

PEACH-APPLE COBBLER WITH WHIPPED CINNAMON SAUCE

CRUST

- 2 cups all-purpose flour
- 1 teaspoon salt
- ⅔ cup vegetable shortening
- ½ cup plus 1 tablespoon cold water

FILLING

- 2½ cups peeled, cored, and chopped tart cooking apples (about 3 apples)
- 1 package (16 ounces) frozen unsweetened peach slices, thawed and undrained
- 2 cups granulated sugar
- ½ cup chopped walnuts
- ¼ cup all-purpose flour
- ½ teaspoon ground cinnamon
- ¼ teaspoon ground nutmeg
- 1 egg, beaten
- 1 tablespoon granulated sugar

SAUCE

- 1 cup whipping cream
- ¼ cup sifted confectioners sugar
- ¼ teaspoon ground cinnamon

For crust, combine flour and salt in a medium bowl. Using a pastry blender or 2 knives, cut in shortening until mixture resembles coarse meal. Sprinkle with water; mix until a soft dough forms. On a lightly floured surface, use a floured rolling pin to roll out dough to ⅛-inch thickness. Reserving dough scraps, cut a 14-inch circle. Transfer to an ungreased 10-inch deep-dish pie plate. Use a sharp knife to cut out about 10 small leaves from dough scraps. Cover all dough pieces; set aside.

For sauce, place a medium bowl and beaters from an electric mixer in freezer until well chilled.

Preheat oven to 425 degrees. For filling, combine apples, peaches, 2 cups sugar, walnuts, flour, cinnamon, and

Topped with Whipped Cinnamon Sauce, Peach-Apple Cobbler is a delectable combination of fruits and nuts.

nutmeg in a large bowl. Pour filling into crust. Fold edges of crust over filling, making overlapping folds every few inches and leaving center of filling uncovered. Brush crust with egg. Place leaves around edges of crust. Brush leaves with egg; sprinkle with 1 tablespoon sugar. Bake 45 to 50 minutes or until crust is golden brown and fruit is tender. If crust becomes too brown, cover with aluminum foil for last 15 to 20 minutes of baking time.

In chilled bowl, whip cream until soft peaks form. Add sugar and cinnamon; beat until stiff peaks form. Place a dollop of sauce in center of cobbler and serve additional sauce with each serving.

Yield: about 12 servings

FRIENDLY FARM ANIMALS

For each animal (pages 102 and 103), you will need instant papier mâché, a plastic foam egg (2¼"h for chicken, 2¾"h for lamb or pig, or 3¾"h for cow), gesso, acrylic paints (see instructions for colors), paintbrushes, matte clear acrylic spray, hot glue gun, glue sticks, and craft knife (optional).
For lamb, you will also need 5" of wired miniature greenery garland and a ½" x 6" torn fabric strip.
For pig, you will also need a black permanent felt-tip pen with fine point and a ½" x 6" torn fabric strip.
For cow, you will also need a ½" cow bell, a ¼" x 10" torn fabric strip, and a small silk holly sprig.

Note: After applying papier mâché features to egg, smooth edges of features onto egg. Allow papier mâché to dry completely before painting. Allow to dry after each coat of gesso or acrylic spray and after each paint color.

CHICKEN
1. Follow manufacturer's instructions to mix papier mâché with water. Apply a ⅛" thick layer of papier mâché over egg; flatten large end of egg for bottom.
2. Form a ¼" long beak and a ¼"h comb from papier mâché; apply to egg.
3. Apply 2 coats of gesso to chicken.
4. Paint chicken cream, beak yellow, and comb red. Paint black eyes; paint black spots on bottom half of chicken.
5. Spray chicken with acrylic spray.
6. For place card holder (page 104), use craft knife to cut a ½" deep slit in back of egg. Insert place card into slit.

LAMB
1. Follow Step 1 of Chicken instructions.
2. Form a ¼" long muzzle and two 1" long ears from papier mâché; apply to egg.
3. Apply 2 coats of gesso to lamb.
4. Paint lamb cream. Paint ears and muzzle black. Paint tip of muzzle pink. Paint black eyes.
5. Spray lamb with acrylic spray.
6. For wreath, form a circle from garland; glue to secure. Glue wreath to lamb. Tie fabric strip into a bow; trim ends. Glue bow to wreath.

PIG
1. Follow Step 1 of Chicken instructions.
2. Form a ¼" long muzzle and two ½" long ears from papier mâché; apply to egg.
3. Apply 2 coats of gesso to pig.
4. Paint pig pink. Use pen to draw eyes and nostrils.
5. Spray pig with acrylic spray.
6. Tie fabric strip into a bow; trim ends. Glue bow to pig.

COW
1. Follow Step 1 of Chicken instructions.
2. Form a 1¼"w x ¼" thick muzzle and two 1" long ears from papier mâché; apply to egg.
3. Apply 2 coats of gesso to cow.
4. Paint cow cream and muzzle pink. Paint black eyes, nostrils, and spots.
5. Spray cow with acrylic spray.
6. Tie bell at center of fabric strip; knot ends of strip together. Place on cow just below ears. Glue bell to cow; glue holly sprig to top of bell.

COUNTRY PLACE MATS

For each place mat (page 103), you will need a 13" x 19" piece of canvas fabric, black fabric paint, paintbrush, scrap fabrics for border, thread to match fabrics, and fabric glue.

1. Paint black spots on canvas to resemble cow spots; allow to dry.
2. For border, cut strips of fabric 4"w by desired lengths (we used 2½" to 4" long strips). With right sides together, use a ¼" seam allowance to sew strips together to form two 4" x 15" and two 4" x 21" pieced strips.
3. (*Note:* For Step 3, match right sides of fabrics and use a 1" seam allowance.) Position place mat with long edges at top and bottom. For left border, center 1 long edge of one 15" strip along left edge of place mat. Stitch in place along long edge. Press border to right side. Repeat to sew remaining 15" strip to right edge of place mat and 21" strips to top and bottom edges of place mat.
4. Press raw edges of border 1" to wrong side; press 1" to wrong side again and glue in place.

BARN

For barn (page 102), you will need a purchased wooden barn (ours is 8" tall), red and yellow acrylic paint, paintbrushes, scrap fabrics, and paper-backed fusible web.

1. Paint barn and roof vent red and roof yellow; allow to dry.
2. Follow manufacturer's instructions to fuse web to wrong sides of fabrics.
3. For roof, cut desired size fabric pieces; fuse pieces to roof, trimming to fit if necessary. For door, cut desired size fabric piece; fuse to barn. Cut fabric strips for trim on door; fuse to barn.

HAYSTACKS

For each haystack (page 102), you will need a 6"h plastic foam egg, a craft hay bale, and craft glue.

1. Use a knife to cut 1" from large end of egg for bottom.
2. Crumble hay bale into a large bowl.
3. Apply a thick coat of glue to egg and roll in hay, completely covering egg. Allow to dry.

NEW YEAR'S COUNTDOWN

Ring out the old and ring in the new with a lively pasta party! Guests will revel in the spirit of camaraderie as they sample an assortment of flavorful new sauces and tasty pastas. To set the scene for the midnight countdown, clocks of all shapes and sizes are arranged with glowing candles. Little clocks also appear on the timely invitations, favors, and napkin rings. For festive favors, miniature top hats hold party horns, confetti, and champagne flutes for toasting in the New Year.

Basil-Olive Oil Spread
Hearts of Lettuce with Caesar Dressing
Alfredo Mushroom Sauce
Marinara Sauce
Spinach Pasta Sauce
Coconut Baklava
Sparkling Lime Spritzer

SPARKLING LIME SPRITZER

2 cups boiling water
¼ cup lime-flavored gelatin
1 liter dry white wine
1 cup vodka
2 tablespoons lime juice
1 liter ginger ale, chilled

    Fresh lime slices and maraschino cherries on wooden skewers to garnish

In a small bowl, combine water and gelatin; stir until gelatin dissolves. In a 3-quart container, combine gelatin mixture, wine, vodka, and lime juice. Cover and refrigerate until well chilled. Stir in ginger ale. Serve over ice. Garnish with lime slices and cherries.

Yield: about fifteen 6-ounce servings

HEARTS OF LETTUCE WITH CAESAR DRESSING

DRESSING
1⅔ cups olive oil
1 cup (4 ounces) shredded Parmesan cheese
⅔ cup white wine vinegar
1 tube (1¾ ounces) anchovy paste
2 tablespoons lemon juice
3 cloves garlic, minced
2 teaspoons Worcestershire sauce
1 teaspoon salt
1 teaspoon ground black pepper
½ teaspoon dry mustard

CROUTONS
1 cup butter or margarine
1 teaspoon garlic powder
½ teaspoon salt
½ loaf French bread, cut into cubes (about 4¾ cups)

SALAD
2 heads iceberg lettuce
8 green onions

8 cherry tomatoes, halved
Fresh parsley

For dressing, combine all ingredients in a 2-pint jar with a tight fitting lid. Shake until well blended. Refrigerate 8 hours or overnight to allow flavors to blend.

For croutons, preheat oven to 350 degrees. In a large skillet, combine butter, garlic powder, and salt. Cook over medium heat until butter melts. Stir in bread cubes. Spread evenly in a jellyroll pan. Stirring occasionally, bake 20 to 25 minutes or until bread is golden brown. Transfer to paper towels to cool completely.

For salad, cut heads of lettuce lengthwise into eight 1-inch slices. Place slices of lettuce on individual plates. Arrange green onions, tomatoes, and parsley on lettuce. Pour dressing over salads. Sprinkle croutons over salads.

Yield: 8 servings

BASIL-OLIVE OIL SPREAD

1⅓ cups chicken broth
1 cup plain bread crumbs
2 tablespoons dried basil leaves
1½ cups olive oil
1 cup finely chopped fresh parsley
6 cloves garlic, minced
1 teaspoon salt
1 teaspoon ground black pepper
2 loaves (1 pound each) French bread to serve

In a medium bowl, combine broth, bread crumbs, and basil; let stand 30 minutes. Stir in oil, parsley, garlic, salt, and pepper. Cover and refrigerate 8 hours or overnight to allow flavors to blend. Spread on slices of French bread.

Yield: about 3 cups sauce

SPINACH PASTA SAUCE

½ cup butter or margarine
1 onion, chopped
2 cloves garlic, minced
5 tablespoons all-purpose flour
2 packages (10 ounces each) frozen chopped spinach, thawed and well drained
⅓ cup shredded Parmesan cheese
¼ cup chopped fresh basil leaves *or* 2 teaspoons dried basil leaves
1 teaspoon salt
1 teaspoon ground black pepper
2 cans (14½ ounces each) chicken broth
½ cup whipping cream
4 packages (9 ounces each) refrigerated cheese-filled tortellini, cooked according to package directions, to serve

In a Dutch oven, melt butter over medium heat. Add onion and garlic; cook until onion is tender. Stir in flour; cook 1 minute. Stir in next 5 ingredients. Gradually stir in broth and cream. Stirring constantly, bring to a boil and cook until thickened. Serve warm over tortellini.

Yield: 10 to 12 servings

ALFREDO MUSHROOM SAUCE

½ cup butter or margarine
½ cup chopped green onions
3 cloves garlic, minced
1 teaspoon salt
½ teaspoon ground black pepper
2 tablespoons all-purpose flour
8 ounces fresh mushrooms, sliced
2 cups whipping cream, warmed
1 cup shredded Parmesan cheese
1 pound spinach fettucine, cooked according to package directions, to serve

In a large skillet, melt butter over medium heat. Add onions, garlic, salt, and pepper; cook until onions are tender. Stir in flour; cook 1 minute. Add mushrooms; cook until all liquid has evaporated. Gradually stir in cream and cheese. Stirring constantly, bring to a boil and cook until thickened. Serve warm over fettucine.

Yield: 8 to 10 servings

MARINARA SAUCE

- ¼ cup olive oil
- 1 cup finely chopped sweet red pepper
- 1 onion, finely chopped
- 2 cloves garlic, minced
- 1 can (29 ounces) tomato sauce
- 1 can (14½ ounces) Italian-style stewed tomatoes, undrained
- 1 can (6 ounces) tomato paste
- 2 teaspoons salt
- 1 teaspoon dried parsley flakes
- 1 teaspoon granulated sugar
- ½ teaspoon dried oregano leaves
- ½ teaspoon dried basil leaves
- ½ teaspoon dried thyme leaves
- ¼ teaspoon ground black pepper
- 1½ pounds bow tie pasta, cooked according to package directions, to serve

In a large saucepan, combine oil, red pepper, onion, and garlic. Cook over medium heat until onion is tender. Add next 10 ingredients; stir until well blended. Bring to a boil, reduce heat to low, cover, and simmer 1 hour. Serve warm over bow tie pasta.

Yield: 10 to 12 servings

Clockwise from left: Alfredo Mushroom Sauce, Marinara Sauce, and Spinach Pasta Sauce are served with a variety of pastas. Shown on page 108: Begin your meal with Hearts of Lettuce with Caesar Dressing and slices of French bread topped with Basil-Olive Oil Spread. Sparkling Lime Spritzers are cool and refreshing.

COCONUT BAKLAVA

1 can (14 ounces) sweetened
    condensed milk
1 cup quick-cooking rolled oats
1 cup sweetened shredded coconut
1 cup finely chopped pecans
½ cup firmly packed brown sugar
1 package (3 ounces) cream cheese,
    softened
½ teaspoon ground cinnamon
¼ teaspoon ground allspice
1 package (16 ounces) frozen
    phyllo pastry, thawed
    according to package directions
    Butter-flavored vegetable cooking
    spray
1 cup granulated sugar
½ cup water
¼ cup honey

In a large bowl, combine milk, oats, coconut, pecans, brown sugar, cream cheese, cinnamon, and allspice.

Preheat oven to 350 degrees. With all sheets of pastry layered together, cut pastry into an 8½ x 12½-inch rectangle. Spray each sheet with cooking spray. Place 7 pastry sheets in a greased 9 x 13-inch baking pan. Spoon ½ of coconut mixture evenly over pastry. Place 7 pastry sheets over coconut mixture. Repeat with remaining coconut mixture and pastry. Use a sharp knife to cut baklava into a diamond pattern. Bake 40 to 45 minutes or until golden brown. Cool completely in pan.

In a small saucepan, combine sugar, water, and honey. Bring to a boil, reduce heat to low, and simmer 5 minutes. Pour syrup over pastry. Cover and let stand at room temperature 24 hours. Store in an airtight container in refrigerator.

Yield: about 2 dozen pieces pastry

Flaky phyllo pastry is layered with a sweet, nutty filling to create Coconut Baklava. The Clock Napkin Rings are dressed up with elegant black bow ties.

CLOCK FAVORS, INVITATIONS, AND NAPKIN RINGS

For each favor (page 113), you will need a 2½" square and a 4½" square of gold wrapping paper, a 4½" square each of red wrapping paper and poster board, 9¼" of ⅛" dia. twisted gold cord, 6" of ⅛"w gold trim, copier paper, tracing paper, black paper, 1 brass paper fastener, craft glue, craft knife, compass, and spray adhesive.

For each invitation (page 113), you will need a Clock Favor, a 5⅜" x 7¼" stationery card, a black calligraphy pen, and craft glue.

For each napkin ring (this page), you will need a Clock Favor, a napkin ring, 8" of ⅞"w and 1" of ¼"w black satin ribbon, black thread, hot glue gun, and glue sticks.

CLOCK FAVOR

1. Photocopy clock face, page 122, onto copier paper; cut out.

2. (*Note:* Use spray adhesive for gluing unless otherwise indicated.) Glue poster board square to wrong side of 4½″ gold paper square.

3. Use compass to draw a 1½″ dia. circle on remaining gold paper, a 3¼″ dia. circle on red paper, and a 3½″ dia. circle on paper-covered poster board; cut out.

4. Glue clock face to center of red circle; glue small gold circle to center of clock face. Cut a small hole through center of clock face.

5. Use craft glue to glue trim along edge of small gold circle and cord along edge of clock face; trim to fit. Allow to dry.

6. For clock hands, trace patterns, page 122, onto tracing paper; cut out. Use patterns to cut hands from black paper.

7. Insert fastener through holes of clock hands and face; bend tabs apart.

8. Glue clock face to center of large gold circle.

INVITATION

1. Use craft glue to glue clock favor to center of card; allow to dry.

2. Use pen to write "Out with the old … In with the new" on card.

NAPKIN RINGS

1. For bow tie, cut a 3¾″ length of ⅞″w ribbon. Overlap ends ¼″ and tack together to form a loop. With overlap at center, flatten loop. Repeat with remaining ⅞″w ribbon. Matching centers, place small loop on large loop. Baste across center of loops. Pull basting thread, drawing up gathers; knot thread and trim ends. Wrap ¼″w ribbon around center of loops; tack in place.

2. Hot glue bow tie to bottom of clock favor. Hot glue favor to napkin ring.

The clever Clock Invitations joyfully herald the New Year, and Clock Favors help count down the minutes till midnight. Confetti Glasses are colorfully decorated using an easy, temporary technique.

CONFETTI GLASSES

For each glass (this page), you will need a clear glass with straight sides, clear self-adhesive plastic (Con-tact® paper), confetti, and craft knife.

Note: This technique provides a temporary decoration for everyday glasses that can be removed after use.

1. Measure around widest part of glass; add 1″. Measure height of glass. Cut a piece of plastic the determined measurements.

2. Remove paper backing and place plastic with adhesive side up. Sprinkle confetti onto plastic.

3. With 1 long edge of plastic along bottom edge of glass, wrap plastic around glass, smoothing bubbles or wrinkles.

4. Use craft knife to trim edges of plastic at top and bottom of glass, forming straight edges. Peel excess plastic from glass.

PATTERNS

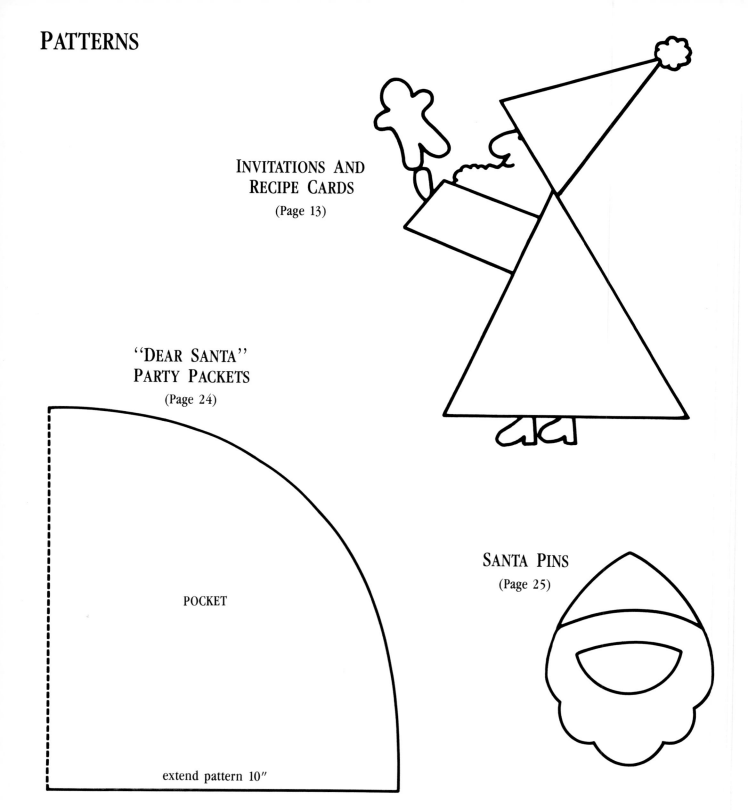

INVITATIONS AND
RECIPE CARDS

(Page 13)

"DEAR SANTA"
PARTY PACKETS

(Page 24)

POCKET

extend pattern 10"

SANTA PINS

(Page 25)

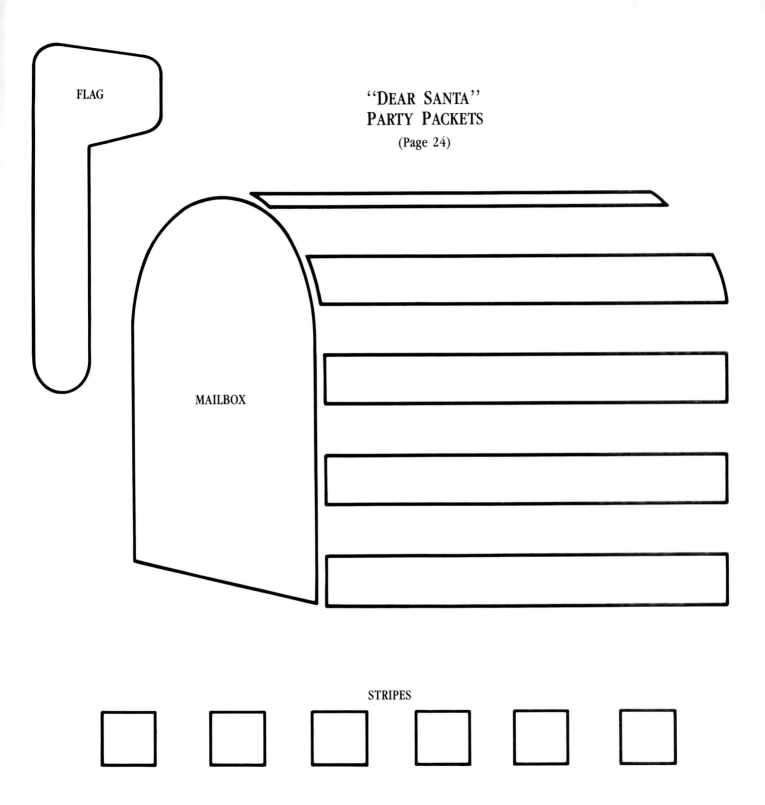

FLAG

"DEAR SANTA"
PARTY PACKETS

(Page 24)

MAILBOX

STRIPES

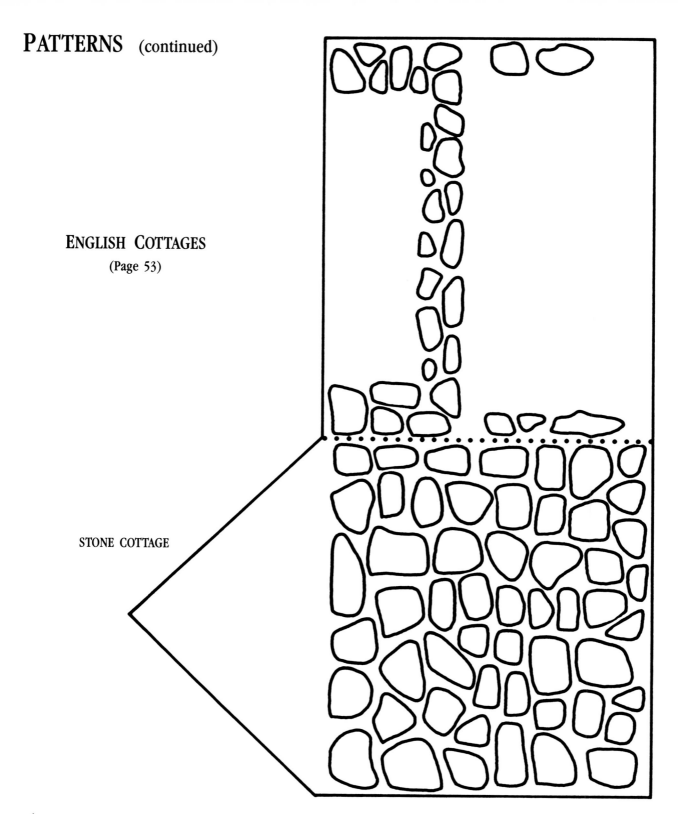

ENGLISH COTTAGES

(Page 53)

STONE COTTAGE

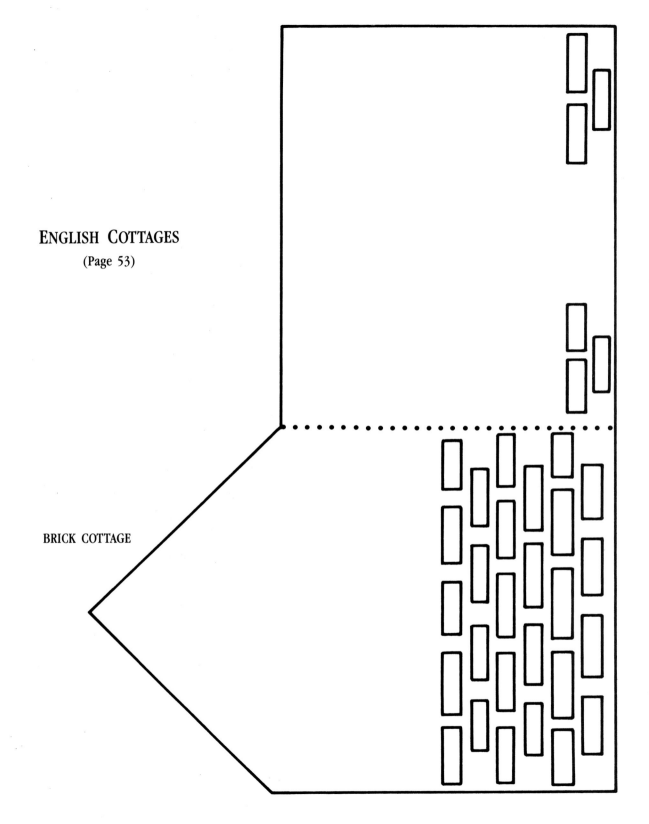

ENGLISH COTTAGES

(Page 53)

BRICK COTTAGE

PATTERNS (continued)

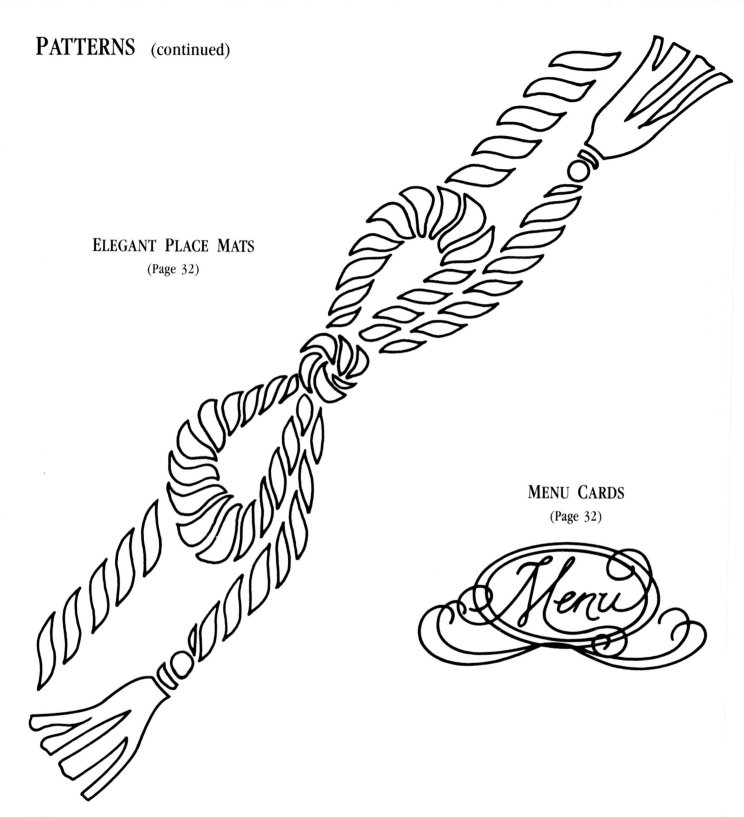

ELEGANT PLACE MATS

(Page 32)

MENU CARDS

(Page 32)

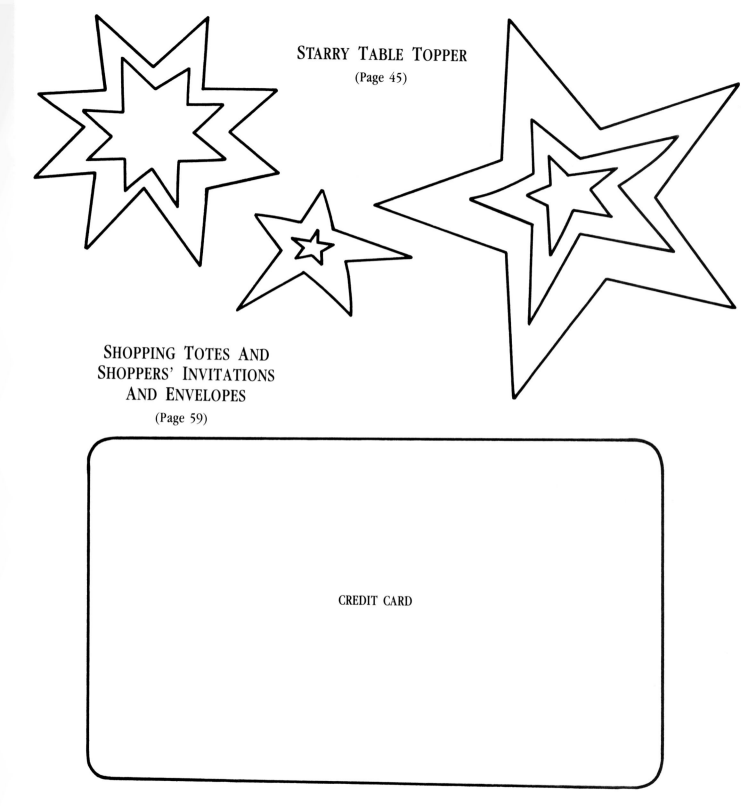

STARRY TABLE TOPPER
(Page 45)

SHOPPING TOTES AND
SHOPPERS' INVITATIONS
AND ENVELOPES
(Page 59)

CREDIT CARD

PATTERNS (continued)

PAINTING KITS
AND PAINTED PAPER

(Page 39)

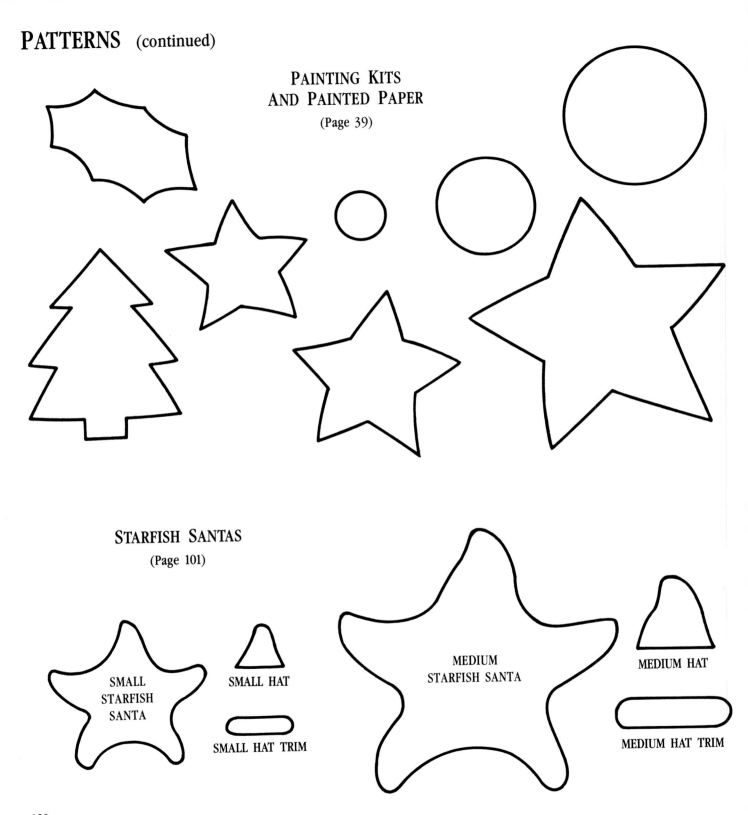

STARFISH SANTAS

(Page 101)

SMALL
STARFISH
SANTA

SMALL HAT

SMALL HAT TRIM

MEDIUM
STARFISH SANTA

MEDIUM HAT

MEDIUM HAT TRIM

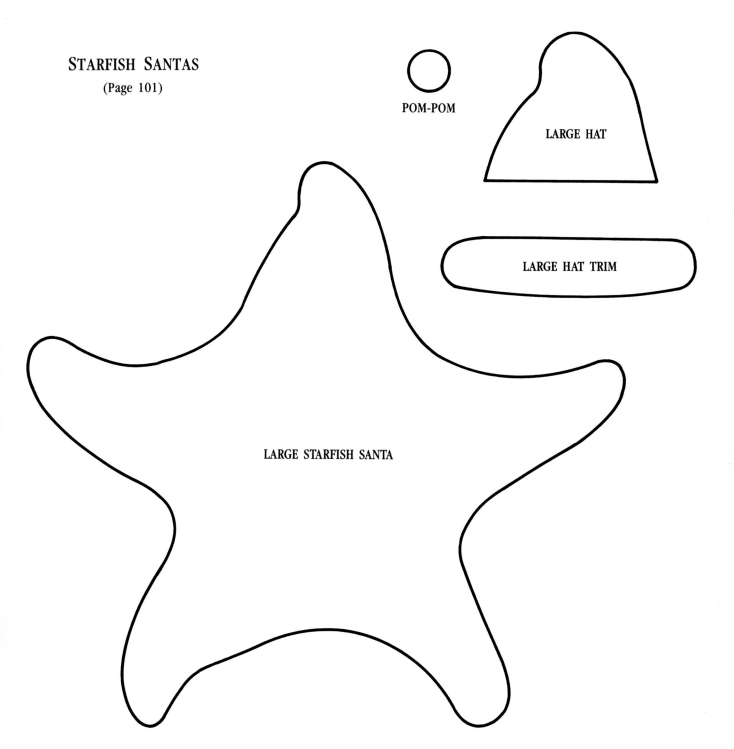

STARFISH SANTAS

(Page 101)

POM-POM

LARGE HAT

LARGE HAT TRIM

LARGE STARFISH SANTA

121

PATTERNS (continued)

WATERMELON SANTAS

(Page 84)

NAPKIN TIES

(Page 84)

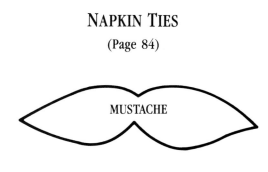

MUSTACHE

MITTEN

CLOCK FAVORS, INVITATIONS, AND NAPKIN RINGS

(Page 112)

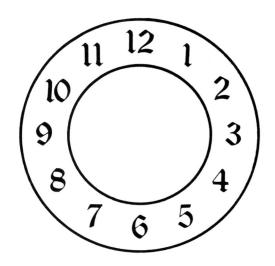

GENERAL INSTRUCTIONS

TRACING PATTERNS

When one-half of pattern (indicated by dashed line on pattern) is shown, fold tracing paper in half and place fold along dashed line of pattern. Trace pattern half, including all placement symbols and markings; turn folded paper over and draw over all markings. Unfold pattern and lay flat. Cut out pattern.

When entire pattern is shown, place tracing paper over pattern and trace pattern, including all placement symbols and markings. Cut out pattern.

STENCILING

1. For stencil, cut a piece of acetate 1″ larger on all sides than entire pattern. Center acetate over pattern and use permanent felt-tip pen with fine point to trace pattern. Place acetate piece on cutting mat and use craft knife to cut out stencil, making sure edges are smooth.
2. (*Note:* If desired, use removable tape to mask any cutout areas on stencil next to area being painted.) Hold or tape stencil in place. Use a clean, dry stencil brush for each color of paint. Dip brush in paint and remove excess on a paper towel. Brush should be almost dry to produce good results. Beginning at edge of cutout area, apply paint in a stamping motion. If desired, shade design by stamping additional paint around edge of cutout area. Carefully remove stencil and allow paint to dry.

CROSS STITCH

COUNTED CROSS STITCH (X)

Work 1 Cross Stitch to correspond to each colored square in the chart. For horizontal rows, work stitches in 2 journeys (Fig. 1). For vertical rows, complete each stitch as shown in Fig. 2. When the chart shows a Backstitch crossing a colored square (Fig. 3), a Cross Stitch (Fig. 1 or 2) should be worked first; then the Backstitch (Fig. 5) should be worked on top of the Cross Stitch.

Fig. 1

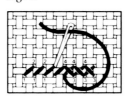

Fig. 2

Fig. 3

QUARTER STITCH (¼ X)

Quarter Stitches are denoted by triangular shapes of color in the chart and color key. Come up at 1 (Fig. 4); then split fabric thread to go down at 2.

Fig. 4

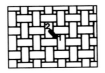

BACKSTITCH (B'ST)

For outline detail, Backstitch (shown in chart and color key by black or colored straight lines) should be worked after the design has been completed (Fig. 5).

Fig. 5

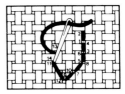

FRENCH KNOT

Bring needle up at 1. Wrap thread once around needle and insert needle at 2, holding end of thread with non-stitching fingers (Fig. 6). Tighten knot; then pull needle through fabric, holding thread until it must be released. For a larger knot, use more strands; wrap only once.

Fig. 6

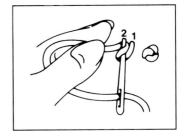

KITCHEN TIPS

MEASURING INGREDIENTS

Liquid measuring cups have a rim above the measuring line to keep liquid ingredients from spilling. Nested measuring cups are used to measure dry ingredients, butter, shortening, and peanut butter. Measuring spoons are used for measuring both dry and liquid ingredients.

To measure flour or granulated sugar: Spoon ingredient into nested measuring cup and level off with a knife. Do not pack down with spoon.

To measure confectioners sugar: Sift sugar, spoon lightly into nested measuring cup, and level off with a knife.

To measure brown sugar: Pack sugar into nested measuring cup and level off with a knife. Sugar should hold its shape when removed from cup.

To measure dry ingredients equaling less than ¼ cup: Dip measuring spoon into ingredient and level off with a knife.

To measure butter, shortening, or peanut butter: Pack ingredient firmly into nested measuring cup and level off with a knife.

To measure liquids: Use a liquid measuring cup placed on a flat surface. Pour ingredient into cup and check measuring line at eye level.

To measure honey or syrup: For more accurate measurement, lightly spray measuring cup or spoon with cooking spray before measuring so the liquid will release easily from cup or spoon.

TESTS FOR CANDY MAKING

To determine the correct temperature of cooked candy, use a candy thermometer and the cold water test. Before each use, check the accuracy of your candy thermometer by attaching it to the side of a small saucepan of water, making sure thermometer does not touch bottom of pan. Bring water to a boil. Thermometer should register 212 degrees when water begins to boil. If it does not, adjust the temperature range for each candy consistency accordingly.

When using a candy thermometer, insert thermometer into candy mixture, making sure thermometer does not touch bottom of pan. Read temperature at eye level. Cook candy to desired temperature range. Working quickly, drop about ½ teaspoon of candy mixture into a cup of ice water. Use a fresh cup of water for each test. Use the following descriptions to determine if candy has reached the correct consistency:

Soft Ball Stage (234 to 240 degrees): Candy can be rolled into a soft ball in ice water but will flatten when held in your hand.

Firm Ball Stage (242 to 248 degrees): Candy can be rolled into a firm ball in ice water but will flatten if pressed when removed from the water.

Hard Ball Stage (250 to 268 degrees): Candy can be rolled into a hard ball in ice water and will remain hard when removed from the water.

Soft Crack Stage (270 to 290 degrees): Candy will form hard threads in ice water but will soften when removed from the water.

Hard Crack Stage (300 to 310 degrees): Candy will form brittle threads in ice water and will remain brittle when removed from the water.

SOFTENING BUTTER OR MARGARINE

To soften butter, remove wrapper from butter and place on a microwave-safe plate. Microwave 1 stick 20 to 30 seconds at medium-low power (30%).

SOFTENING CREAM CHEESE

To soften cream cheese, remove wrapper from cream cheese and place on a microwave-safe plate. Microwave 1 to 1½ minutes at medium power (50%) for one 8-ounce package or 30 to 45 seconds for one 3-ounce package.

SUBSTITUTING HERBS

To substitute fresh herbs for dried, use 1 tablespoon fresh chopped herbs for ½ teaspoon dried herbs.

WHIPPING CREAM

For greatest volume, chill a glass bowl, beaters, and cream until well chilled before whipping. In warm weather, place chilled bowl over ice while whipping cream.

CUTTING COOKIE SHAPES

To cut out cookie shapes, dip cookie cutter in flour to keep dough from sticking to cutter.

BEATING EGG WHITES

For greatest volume, beat egg whites at room temperature in a clean, dry metal or glass bowl.

SHREDDING CHEESE

To shred cheese easily, place wrapped cheese in freezer for 10 to 20 minutes before shredding.

ROLLING OUT PIE DOUGH

Tear off four 24-inch-long pieces of plastic wrap. Overlapping long edges, place two pieces of wrap on a slightly damp, flat surface; smooth out wrinkles. Place dough in center of wrap. Overlapping long edges, use remaining pieces of wrap to cover dough. Use rolling pin to roll out dough 2 inches larger than diameter of pie plate. Remove top pieces of wrap. Invert dough into pie plate. Remove remaining pieces of wrap.

MELTING CHOCOLATE

To melt chocolate, place chopped or shaved chocolate in top of a double boiler (or in a heat-proof bowl over a saucepan of water) over hot, not boiling, water. Stir occasionally until melted. Remove from heat and use for dipping as desired. If necessary, chocolate may be returned to heat to remelt.

TOASTING NUTS

To toast nuts, spread nuts on an ungreased baking sheet. Stirring occasionally, bake 8 to 10 minutes in a preheated 350-degree oven until nuts are slightly darker in color.

TOASTING COCONUT

To toast coconut, spread a thin layer of coconut on an ungreased baking sheet. Stirring occasionally, bake 5 to 7 minutes in a preheated 350-degree oven until coconut is light brown.

EQUIVALENT MEASUREMENTS

1 tablespoon	=	3 teaspoons
⅛ cup (1 fluid ounce)	=	2 tablespoons
¼ cup (2 fluid ounces)	=	4 tablespoons
⅓ cup	=	5⅓ tablespoons
½ cup (4 fluid ounces)	=	8 tablespoons
¾ cup (6 fluid ounces)	=	12 tablespoons
1 cup (8 fluid ounces)	=	16 tablespoons or ½ pint
2 cups (16 fluid ounces)	=	1 pint
1 quart (32 fluid ounces)	=	2 pints
½ gallon (64 fluid ounces)	=	2 quarts
1 gallon (128 fluid ounces)	=	4 quarts

HELPFUL FOOD EQUIVALENTS

½ cup butter	=	1 stick butter
1 square baking chocolate	=	1 ounce chocolate
1 cup chocolate chips	=	6 ounces chocolate chips
2¼ cups packed brown sugar	=	1 pound brown sugar
3½ cups unsifted confectioners sugar	=	1 pound confectioners sugar
2 cups granulated sugar	=	1 pound granulated sugar
4 cups all-purpose flour	=	1 pound all-purpose flour
1 cup shredded cheese	=	4 ounces cheese
3 cups sliced carrots	=	1 pound carrots
½ cup chopped celery	=	1 rib celery
½ cup chopped onion	=	1 medium onion
1 cup chopped green pepper	=	1 large green pepper

RECIPE INDEX

127

CREDITS

We want to extend a warm thank you to the generous people who allowed us to photograph our projects in their homes:

Merry Cookie Swap: John and Anne Childs
Christmas in the Forest: John and Anne Childs
Wintry Elegance: Dr. Dan and Sandra Cook

A Splendid Twelfth Night: Mrs. Shirley Held
Christmas Picnic: John and Anne Childs

We also thank the Little Rock Skating Arena in Little Rock, Arkansas, for allowing us to photograph our *"Just for Kids" Skating Party* at the arena.

A special word of thanks goes to Hill Design in Concord, New Hampshire, for the use of the Brown Bag Cookie Art ceramic ''Santa in Sleigh'' cookie mold that was used to create the *Santa Cookie* shown on page 66.

To Magna IV Color Imaging of Little Rock, Arkansas, we say thank you for the superb color reproduction and excellent pre-press preparation.

We want to especially thank photographers Mark Mathews, Ken West, Larry Pennington, and Karen Busick Shirey of Peerless Photography, Little Rock, Arkansas, and Jerry R. Davis of Jerry Davis Photography, Little Rock, Arkansas, for their time, patience, and excellent work.

To the talented people who helped in the creation of the following recipes and projects in this book, we extend a special word of thanks:

Sesame Cookies, page 13: Glenda Warren
Mocha-Carrot Cake, page 68: Leslye Boyce
Onion-Cheese Casserole, page 91: Florence Morris

Corn Bread Salad, page 105: Nora Faye Spencer Clift
Sugar and Spice design, page 71: Jane Chandler

We extend a sincere thank you to the people who assisted in making and testing the projects in this book: Karen Brogan, Mary Hicks, Kathy Jones, Patricia Keightley, Patricia O'Neil, Opal Steen, and Karen Tyler.